PLANNING THE FUTURE FOR A SPECIAL NEEDS CHILD

A PARENT'S GUIDE TO SPECIAL NEEDS PLANNING AT EACH STAGE OF THEIR LOVED ONE'S LIFE

KERRIE A. LLOYD, ChSNC®

© **Copyright January 5, 2023 - All rights reserved.**

The content contained within this book may not be reproduced, duplicated or transmitted without direct written permission from the author or the publisher.

Under no circumstances will any blame or legal responsibility be held against the publisher, or author, for any damages, reparation, or monetary loss due to the information contained within this book. Either directly or indirectly. You are responsible for your own choices, actions, and results.

Legal Notice:

This book is copyright protected. This book is only for personal use. You cannot amend, distribute, sell, use, quote or paraphrase any part, or the content within this book, without the consent of the author or publisher.

Disclaimer Notice:

Please note the information contained within this document is for educational and entertainment purposes only. All effort has been executed to present accurate, up to date, and reliable, complete information. No warranties of any kind are declared or implied. Readers acknowledge that the author is not engaging in the rendering of legal, financial, medical or professional advice. The content within this book has been derived from various sources. Please consult a licensed professional before attempting any techniques outlined in this book.

By reading this document, the reader agrees that under no circumstances is the author responsible for any losses, direct or indirect, which are incurred as a result of the use of the information contained within this document, including, but not limited to, — errors, omissions, or inaccuracies.

CONTENTS

Introduction	7
1. HELP YOURSELF TO HELP YOUR CHILD	15
Effective Stress Management For Parents Of A Child With Special Needs	18
Why Parenting A Child With Special Needs Is Stressful	31
How To Manage Stress Related To Parenting A Child With Special Needs	32
How Can I Help My Child? Where Do I Go From Here?	37
2. NOTICING DIFFERENCES AND LEARNING TO COPE IN THE FIRST THREE YEARS	45
What Are Some Common Signs That A Child Has Special Needs?	48
After You Find Out That Your Child Has A Disability	56
Discussing Your Child's Disability With Them	66
3. GAINING CONFIDENCE IN PRESCHOOL AND EARLY ELEMENTARY	75
Building Confidence In a Child With Special Needs	76
Helping Your Child Through Preschool And Early Elementary	83
No Child Left Behind	86

4. MAKING PROGRESS IN EARLY
   ELEMENTARY AND MIDDLE
   SCHOOL   97
   What Is Special Education?   99
   What's An IEP?   100
   What's The Referral And Evaluation
   Process?   102
   How Is An IEP Developed?   105
   What Are My Legal Rights?   107
   What Else Do I Need To Know?   108
   Speech-Language Therapy: What Is It?   109
   What, Your Child May Need Speech-
   Language Therapy?   113
   What's The Law?   115

5. SHINING BRIGHT IN MIDDLE AND
   HIGH SCHOOL   125
   Conservatorship Or Supported Decision-
   Making   128
   How Supported Decision-Making Works   130
   Types Of Supported Decision-Making   133
   How To Set Up Supported Decision-
   Making For Your Child With Special
   Needs   137
   How To Support Your Child With
   Decisions At Any Age   138
   Self-Determination And Children With
   Special Needs   142
   How Are Skills In Self-Determination
   Built?   144
   How Can Families Encourage And
   Support Self-Determination?   144
   Tips For Family To Promote Self
   Determination   146

6. A GENTLE TRANSITION FROM
   SCHOOL TO ADULTHOOD ... 151
   A Guide To Special Needs Guardianship:
   When Your Child Requires Additional
   Levels Of Support ... 160
   Why Is A Guardian Needed For A Person
   With Special Needs? ... 162
   What Are The Powers Of A Guardian? ... 163
   How Is A Guardian For A Special Needs
   Person Chosen? ... 164
   Government Benefits For People With
   Special Needs ... 165
   Transition Services For Adults ... 171
   Transition Planning For Students With
   Special Needs ... 173
   18+ Or Transition Services You Might
   Find In Your Child's School District ... 174

7. ACHIEVING INDEPENDENCE AS AN
   ADULT ... 179
   What Parents Should Know When A
   Child With Special Needs Turns 22 ... 180
   Ageing Out Of Eligibility For Special
   Education ... 185
   Housing Options For Adults With Special
   Needs ... 188
   Financial Planning For Your Loved One
   With Special Needs ... 194

8. WARRIOR PARENTS ... 205

   Conclusion ... 217
   The Big Leap Forward ... 221
   About the Author ... 225
   Resources ... 229

INTRODUCTION

I made the decision to write this book based on the life lessons I have discovered in response to my son Adam's dual diagnosis of autism and deafness. It's interesting that I graduated as a Doctor of Natural Health, NhD before Adam was born. I earned the distinction while reaping the rewards of my career in financial services.

Adam is an amazing individual who happened to be born deaf. He underwent cochlear implant surgery at the age of 2 to improve his communication abilities. Adam is also an individual who was diagnosed with autism at the age of 2½. I had read studies that American Sign Language (ASL) was impactful for autism as well as deafness as a bridge to spoken language. As a result, we shifted to that modality while he learned to communicate. This was the first modality decision we made when developing Adam's long-term plan for the future.

Planning for any child with special needs is difficult. When discovering options for Adam, I realized that the naturalistic approaches I had learned about in the Doctor of Natural Health (NhD) program were also the most effective ones for Adam. An all-natural lifestyle was the second modality decision I made for Adam and it ultimately benefitted the health and wellbeing of the entire family. It wasn't a coincidence that Adam needed me to carry out exactly what I learned in the NhD curriculum before his birth as part of the treatment plan.

Adam's dual diagnosis at birth was likewise not a coincidence. ASL works just as well for the deaf community as a bridge toward spoken language as for those with autism. Due to Adam's dual diagnosis, we were able to get the resources that would eventually allow him to communicate more quickly. This is what we discovered as we planned for Adam's specific requirements at the early educational stage of his life journey. His present-day capacity for interaction, education, and need fulfillment is nothing short of a miracle as a result of the intervention he received.

While learning about Adam's rights under Early Start and the Individuals with Disabilities Education Act

(IDEA), his educational team and I developed an integrated plan for him as a toddler that included holistic therapies we were utilizing at home. Enabling consistency across environments is of ultimate importance to the overall success of intervention. This is what is referred to as "collaboration across environments for fidelity of implementation".

Our first goal was to address environmental factors that, among other things, lead to the escalation of behaviors that are typical of autism. Our second goal was to encourage Adam's curiosity about learning through his educational setting so that he might achieve developmental milestones that would ultimately benefit him and improve his overall quality of life. Our third goal was to establish protocols at home and in the community to generalize skills he gained through intervention.

Adam's physical, mental, and spiritual bodies are treated holistically. We were unable to address one need while ignoring others. Adam is balanced and highly functional, like a typical deaf person when his mind, body, and soul are in harmony. However, when Adam is out of sync, there are symptoms of escalation that, if not addressed, can lead to a catastrophic meltdown. This emphasizes how crucial planning is to overcome the difficulties of each life stage discussed in this book.

Adam's diagnosis acts as a thermometer to highlight life areas that require change. To eliminate, or at least lessen, maladaptive behaviors that are typical of autism, factors that cause behaviors must be addressed. The benefits of these environmental changes have greatly enhanced the quality of life for the entire family. As a result, I am able to understand why Adam is here, and I am content to evolve with him as we journey through every phase of his beautiful life together.

The difficulties I faced as a parent of a child with special needs is greater than I ever imagined. But the rewards are exponential to that. I experienced days feeling completely alone in my struggle and there were other days when I realized Adam and I were meaningful contributors who would ultimately be of service to the special needs community.

It's possible that you've been preoccupied with meeting the demands of your child with special needs and the rest of your family. It is also possible that you haven't had a chance to ask for advice from individuals who have traveled a similar path. I hope you'll find solace in our story as I go through the joys and struggles of raising Adam, regardless of whether you're raising a child who has a variety of physical, developmental, or emotional issues.

It is said that having children will be not only the most difficult but also the most rewarding thing we will ever do. You assume a great deal of responsibility as a parent for the welfare of your child. Your actions and words have an impact on how your child develops and behaves. When your child has unique needs, the job becomes considerably more difficult. Each day brings with it a new set of difficulties and rewards. Your loved ones need your love, support, and direction throughout their life, in both the easy and difficult days. However, with a little help, you can do it and provide your child with excellent care.

Parenting a child with special needs requires a great deal of responsibility and planning. According to census data that can be found at www.census.gov, there is heightened awareness of disability among the adult and elderly population as we age. Yet, it also noted childhood disability warrants attention due to the monetary and nonmonetary cost of care for them.

Studies suggest disability rates among the nation's children have been rising since the early 90's. In fact, the 2019 American Community Survey (ACS) indicates the percentage of children with a disability in the United States increased between 2008 and 2019 from

3.9% to 4.3% with cognitive disability as the most common disability for ages 5 and older. America has a sizable population of individuals with special needs and a growing number of them are our children. This book is written for them and their families with love.

Every parent wants their child to be in good physical and mental health. However, there are those children who lack certain components of health. As parents, we must accept the child and live our own brand of normal rather than resisting the changes required for support. Even though there are certain difficulties, trusting in yourself and your child can help you achieve your goals, which include ensuring the child's happiness.

There are distinct stages of life a neurodiverse loved one will go through, and the diagnosis emphasized in this book is autism spectrum disorders (ASD). The goal of the book, however, is to give all special needs parents a guide to utilize throughout their loved one's life journey so they can plan for a future that is often uncertain.

If you just received, or suspect you will receive, a diagnosis, you're undoubtedly concerned with what happens next. You've given a lot of thought to your child's future as a parent, especially after a formal diagnosis and the planning for the future begins now. Your planning efforts can make a difference for your child and this book will help you map a way forward.

Your ability to help your child will be improved the more you are aware of their needs and the planning challenges at each stage of his or her life. Planning and collaboration are critical to success. Even though it's true that a person does not just "grow out of" special needs, there are a number of things that can be done to help in learning new abilities to overcome a wide range of obstacles. This is where the treatment team comes in, which includes parents and caregivers. If the team implements the treatment plan in a way that provides consistency across environments, the quality of life will be improved for your loved one and anyone else he or she interacts with. "fidelity of implementation" is critical in the planning process.

It is clear from the research, that having a diagnosis does not exclude your child from having friends, dating, attending college, getting married, having children, or having a fulfilling, rewarding profession. Early diagnosis and the use of evidence-based interventions help your child with special needs acquire the skills needed to thrive and succeed as children and adults leading to better results. This too, takes planning.

Children with special needs need to learn skills to become successful adults, just like typically growing children do. It's crucial to note, however, that this process often appears different than what a typical child experiences and it requires planning at each life stage. There is no magic bullet. However, a child or adult with special needs usually responds well when provided a routine that is structured and consistent and who is made to feel supported and understood.

I divided the stages into six stages to simplify your reading as you evolve with your loved one. Your child's needs will change as you advance through each of them together. There are specific planning challenges at each of these stages and I hope the pages that follow will help you plan for the future of your loved one with special needs.

It is easier to take these challenges in stages than to tackle everything all at once. Try to focus on today's challenges first. Meeting the other stages one step at a time.

Last but not least, it is impossible to give from a depleted well. Being emotionally resilient enables you to provide the greatest care possible for your loved one. Although this book offers planning advice that can make raising a child with special needs easier at each stage of his or her life, there is also a chapter on self-care that is written specifically for what I like to call "warrior parents."

1

HELP YOURSELF TO HELP YOUR CHILD

It takes a lot of effort to care for a child with special needs. Having a child with special needs can sometimes make parenting even more taxing on the parents. Almost every area of parenting is more challenging, from helping with education to taking care of your loved one's emotional, developmental, and physical needs. Any parent may feel the effects of all of this as overwhelming.

It's critical to recognize the added stress involved in raising a child with special needs. Aside from a heightened degree of uncertainty about the future, recognizing that you are expected to put in more effort than other parents weighs heavy on your mind. Having to establish and evaluate priorities is required. This is not a challenge you can tackle all at once and this does not make you a bad parent. You simply cannot do everything all at once. This is the reason this book is divided into sections you can tackle at different life stages of your loved one.

As you make progress, you must acknowledge your accomplishments in order to manage the inevitable difficulties. This is a marathon and not a sprint. Self-care is the only way to sustain yourself and give you the strength you will need to stay fit on every level of your being. You must also take care of your own emotional, spiritual, and physical needs in order to enable yourself to effectively help your loved one and other members of your family.

Parenting a child with a disability entails special obligations, challenges, and benefits. It necessitates a greater degree of emotional fortitude, persistence, and creativity. Parents of children with physical, intellectual, or developmental disabilities, such as autism spectrum disorders, spina bifida, or Down syndrome, often encounter profound social prejudices. However, they are motivated by the same (or an even stronger) desire to nurture, protect, and empower their children as parents of children perceived as having normative abilities. When these "invisible" barriers go unnoticed, they can be much more unpleasant.

According to the Global Partnership for Education, children with disabilities continue to be the most disadvantaged group in terms of educational opportunities. They face prejudice not only as a result of their disability but also as a result of a lack of understanding and knowledge about its causes, effects, and stigma. For example, parents who are supporting a child with attention deficit hyperactivity disorder (ADHD) or physical ailments like eyesight or mobility problems may feel overpowered by the difficulties in obtaining the right testing or gaining access to a restroom or play area. The difficulties increase when a child's impairment coincides with societal or cultural stereotypes that are already present about gender, color, religion, or sexual orientation. This has an effect on parents that peers, coworkers, and other people may not completely understand or respect.

Parents of children with disabilities may come with unpleasant limits that perpetuate a sense of exclusion or isolation and raise emotions like anger or grief while they proactively seek information, support, and advocacy for their children. Due to these and other reasons, parents who are looking for support for their children with special needs also have a special need for self-care.

A parent may become bone-tired from caring for a child with special needs. I've learned as a mother that it's important to allow myself space to breathe, to center, to refuel, and to pull myself together. When I am nearly out of gas or running on empty, I can't support or be of much value to my child. The following are some of the behaviors I follow and advise you to think about if

EFFECTIVE STRESS MANAGEMENT FOR PARENTS OF A CHILD WITH SPECIAL NEEDS

How can my husband and I handle all of the challenging emotions and additional stress that come with being parents of a child with special needs? Sometimes the work seems to be too much for us to handle.

I recognize and respect the stress you're under. Even under ideal circumstances, parenting is characterized by a great deal of strain and responsibility. When you add in the extra duties and worries that come with raising a child with special needs, the work can seem truly overwhelming. But we want to give you hope and encouragement. You can handle this and do it well, despite how difficult it may be.

It can be hard to raise children with special needs. While certain situations are more stressful than others, even a moderate learning disability can add complexity to day-to-day life. Thankfully, there are choices for getting assistance and support.

You'll discover in this section why raising a child with special needs is stressful. Additionally, you'll find advice and suggestions for reducing stress through self-care, simplification, and burden-sharing.

your child has special needs. Do not forget you are a special parent with special needs.

Practice morning meditation

You can find stability and tranquility in mindfulness exercises such as meditation or prayer. Meditation in the morning is especially beneficial at that time because it allows you to unwind and approach the day with positivity. There is a ton of research to support the idea that practicing meditation directly enhances wellbeing. This can also be done anytime you are feeling overwhelmed with a need to center yourself.

Simple breathing exercises performed in a peaceful environment will help you to focus and make the remainder of the day easier to handle. Finding a peaceful area to sit and focusing your attention on the internal and outward movement of air with each breath is all that is required. Even just closing your eyes for a moment and practicing breathing exercises with a quick prayer can help at moments of anxiety and stress. Almost immediately, you'll notice that your stress level has decreased.

Reach out for assistance

Never force yourself to handle the difficulties of raising a child with special needs by yourself. Ask your friends and family for help whenever you're feeling anxious or overburdened. Sometimes, just talking about your problems might help you conquer them and put them in perspective. However, it is important to speak with people who are supportive, loving, and kind.

Sometimes unwanted advice can just add to your difficulties and it is important to insulate yourself from negativity. We are already dealing with enough and it is important to insulate ourselves from additional stress. Although it is acceptable for people to be uninformed and well-meaning when offering opinions or advise. Their reactions often bring to light the first lesson a special needs parent will learn. It takes a village, yes, but the village must be equipped with the right people who are skilled at working with a child with special needs and their families.

You may find it easier to cope if you talk about your problems with others who are experiencing the same things. People who have experienced similar challenges as yours may also provide you with some insightful advice. Neighborhood special needs parent support groups and online forums for parents of children with special needs can be useful.

One resource I found that is of particular help for families impacted by autism is the Stanford Autism Center at Stanford Children's Health, formerly at UC Santa Barbara. In particular, the Annual Conference and the Fall Mindfulness Skills for Parents online was especially impactful for me. These resources enabled me to become certified in level one of an evidence-based behavior protocol for Adam where I learned to follow his lead while taking advantage of his natural environment to produce, and maintain, gains for him without regression.

Through resources like this, I became connected with other mothers just like me, who could relate to my challenges. At conferences offering resources and support, we met skilled practitioners who were in a position to validate us and enable us to prioritize our next steps moving forward– one step at a time. Gentleness is the approach here with a loving heart and a boatload of empathy.

Request occasional childcare from someone else

Asking someone to watch your child is not something to be ashamed of. Nobody could ever truly be "on the go" all the time. If you want to prevent burnout, you need to give your body and mind some rest. It should be no problem for friends and family to watch your child while you take a break.

Outside family and friends, it might be hard to find workers willing or able to meet your needs. Once you find skilled workers with availability that matches your needs, think about inviting them to spend time with you and the child to determine goodness of fit. A connection may eventually grow that will enable caregivers to work with you and your family. Once caregivers are in place, the next challenge is to keep them so you can work or at least recharge and reset your energy level.

In California, families may be referred to the county Regional Center for resources. Regional Centers are a source of funding for special needs families that will be discussed later in this book. Under the parent support umbrella, you might be entitled to funding for Respite services, which is a form of limited in home care. Respite is different from childcare because parents are required to secure childcare for their loved ones in order to work. Respite, on the other hand enables you to get the help you need for a break, even if you are not working. In this way, special parents can get the support they need for self-care activities.

Although parents are required to provide for care for their children and pay for in home care while they are working, there may be opportunities for Respite services in California. Parents can either call their local Regional Center directly or ask their doctor for a referral to the local Regional Center. In States outside of California, check your State's Council for Developmental Disabilities (SCDD) to determine what services are available (possibly under the term Self Determination).

The National Respite Care Network also provides comprehensive instructions on how to get assistance finding both in-home and out-of-home respite services. In certain instances, a parent's mental health can improve significantly after just one night off.

Discover activities to enjoy while watching your child

Parents should never stop participating in the activities they enjoy. You can take care of your child and pursue interests that keep you sane at the same time. Make the most of the chance to relax and have fun when you find appropriate care and support for your loved one. My go to activities are centered around mindfulness and physical fitness. I utilize time away to be sure I am in the best position to care for Adam at all times when I am with him.

Adam and I also found activities we could enjoy together. We discovered that he loves the outdoors and loves to walk. Therapeutic experts had also informed me that walking and pushing heavy loads are impactful activities for a child with special needs who are sensory seekers, which Adam was. So, Adam learned to walk as one of his pastime activities and sometimes he pushed his own stroller, that also acted as a walker for him. At first, his gait was unstable, but he learned to take longer walks over time, which is an activity we still enjoy today.

Swimming was another activity Adam enjoyed, but he required a high degree of supervision. He could not master the skill of treading water or holding his breath. Then, he mastered both of those skills. It was not until the age of 18 that we could safely let him independently enjoy the deep end of a pool. But he loved to swim, and we needed to support him. Today, Adam is a good swimmer. Needless to say, it was worth the effort waiting for him to learn how.

Starting with Adam where he was and patiently adding gains to his levels of activity over time has been very rewarding. But we had an army of experts helping us every step of the way. My only prayer at the time was that we would find the right resources for Adam to live the life God intended for him. And those prayers were answered. There are so many beautiful souls who found their way to us to help at just the right time to help us teach Adam the skills he was seeking.

We also found the Shea Center for Therapeutic Riding in San Juan Capistrano. Adam learned to ride a horse with skilled multidisciplinary therapists while his dad and I socialized with other parents on the bleachers. This is how we made some lifelong friends we could share our journey with. Adam has also been featured in articles on therapeutic riding and he is a Rockstar in his own right as a result of that. Needless to say, seeing him featured in academic research is rewarding for both of us.

Another favorite activity we enjoy is travel. We started slow with overnight visits with family. Then we increased that to weekends and longer trips. Once we understood Adam was comfortable in different environments, we were able to identify his preference on locations.

We discovered that Adam benefits from calm, nature-based environments away from home and we started taking short trips to Kauai. It is an understatement to say that so much of his autism is environmental. Since it was impactful, we were able to extend those trips to a week or more over time. Removing environmental "attacks" for Adam on vacation made him enjoy our time away more in ways that are therapeutic for the entire family. Even today, we enjoy our annual trip to Kauai so we can all hit the reset button every summer.

Everyone who knows Adam is so proud of him. More importantly, the activities we have pursued for him have made him proud of himself. He is in an inclusive environment where he is a meaningful contributor to the quality of his own life and an example of hope to others.

Do what brings you happiness

Although you can pursue relaxation and enjoyment together, you probably spend a lot of time and effort entertaining your child with a disability. Making sure your child has the same opportunities as other children, requires time and effort. Stress can have an adverse effect on your health if you are not strict about taking care of yourself also, especially if your child has a long-term impairment or requires constant attention to basic safety requirements.

It's crucial to find ways to rejuvenate, unwind, and enjoy life with your loved one with special needs, but also alone as an individual or couple. Parents may be a patient, kind, and proactive protectors, nurturers, and advocates for their child. But only if they enjoy a calm, relaxed, and refueled family environment. Protect yourself and your relationships.

Make a list of "Fun Things We Would Do If We Had Time". To get started, you may list pursuits like riding a bike, going out to dinner with friends or partners, drawing or writing, watching a movie, getting a massage, taking a stroll outside, or working out.

Explore a teahouse

When you have the opportunity to leave the house, think about visiting a nearby tea shop. Tea is an incredibly calming beverage due to its warmth and physical characteristics. It might prove to be the stress reliever you've been looking for when combined with meditation. Yaupon tea is a particularly alluring alternative because it is recognized for boosting mood and providing the body with vitality.

Sometimes, the best you can do is the local coffee shop and that is fine too. Today, there are so many alternatives to hot or cold beverages that are calming and effective. One of my favorites is chamomile tea, which can be found anywhere. This is just a great way to take a load off, put your feet up, and disconnect from the demands of your life.

Take good care of your body

According to research, physical health and mental wellbeing are intricately linked. You need to be in the greatest physical shape possible if you want to parent with the correct mindset every day. It is easy to say, "maintain a balanced diet", and the benefits are obvious. However, for a special needs parent, we often grab food that is easy to get on the fly.

One way I found to maintain a healthy diet was to follow Adam's lead. He had to be on a gluten free casein free (GF/CF) diet, and I prepared food for him as such. We discovered the book "Special Diets for Special Kids" so I could learn what to cook for him and how to substitute ingredients in recipes for him.

Given the time and effort that went into Adam's diet, I decided to convert the house to a GF/CF environment. This killed two birds with one stone. I was able to be sure Adam would not eat anything that would cause an escalation in his behaviors or make him sick. But also, I was confident I was serving healthy alternatives to myself and the rest of the family. We discovered the benefits of removing additives and chemicals from our food as well as his. In the process, I also lost weight that had been hanging on since childbirth. Following Adam's lead benefited me, and this is part of what he came here to teach me.

Then, moving on to exercise. At first, I went to the gym alone and I still enjoy my yoga in solitude. However, later on, when Adam mastered the ability to at least tread water, I was able to go to the gym and allow Adam to enjoy the pool there with a caregiver so I could work out. By watching others in the pool, he mastered the skill to hold his breath and go under water. Processing this ability took him more time than most people. However, he got there. It is because we included him in activities early in life that we were ultimately able to leave him alone in a pool now without fear he is not able to swim.

I have a saying that I just want to outlive Adam by one day. Aside from diet, the best way to extend your life is through exercise. Given the demands of raising a child with special needs, the only real way to do so is to take advantage of caregivers and the resources your gym might have for you. Take your loved one to the gym with you and a caregiver, if it is at all possible.

Other means of exercise might involve activities you might be able to enjoy with your child. Physical activity helps special needs individuals cope in the same way it helps parents and caregivers. By being creative, you should be able to get your heart rate up in just a small amount of time. The point here is to put yourself, and your loved ones, in a position of activity that could be fun for both of you.

Celebrate your child's progress.

You play a significant part in your child's development as parents and caregivers. While they undoubtedly merit congratulations for achieving their goals, you also merit a round of applause.

Take advantage of these chances to tell yourself how well you are doing. Go out to eat with your family, order your favorite dish, bake your favorite goodie, or do something as easy as going to the park to celebrate. Take an aromatherapy bath.

It is normal to feel lost occasionally. But it's vital to keep in mind that any amount of progress deserves a celebration. We have learned to celebrate the little things as a bridge to greater progress down the road. Remember, neither you nor your child is alone. There is always assistance and help available. Get the help you need and put yourself in a position to help yourself help your loved one.

WHY PARENTING A CHILD WITH SPECIAL NEEDS IS STRESSFUL

Depending on the condition of the parents, the child's impairment, and the specific demands placed on the parent, stress might stem from a variety of problems. Top sources of stress include the following:

- Being overwhelmed by the sheer volume of therapies and other responsibilities that come with parenting a child with disabilities.
- Feeling cut off from other parents and friends.
- Coping with the financial difficulties that can arise from providing therapies or leaving work because of a child with special needs.
- Feeling guilty or depressed about a child's disability.

- Worrying about a child's wellbeing and the future.
- When one parent spends most of their time and energy on the child with special needs, stress can develop within the family.
- The exhaustion that might result from having to care for a child with special needs while still working and maintaining their house.
- Anxiety may contribute to insomnia.

HOW TO MANAGE STRESS RELATED TO PARENTING A CHILD WITH SPECIAL NEEDS

Stress management can be quite challenging when one feels alone and guilty. Lack of both practical and emotional assistance is another factor. Meetings and schedules that are too complicated might be mentally taxing. Thankfully, there are resources and solutions available to assist with all of these problems.

Understanding and Handling Grief and Guilt

Parents do go through a grieving process, and they might feel bad about it. For parents of a child with special needs, grief and guilt are common emotions, but they can also worsen anxiety and depression.

Because grief may recur over time, it's crucial to become adept at identifying and managing it.

Organizing Your Workload

The numerous demands made on parents of child with special needs may leave them feeling exhausted.

Mothers generally appear to feel more overburdened than fathers; hence, the invisible job that women do for the family gets harder. Whether the mother works a full-time job or not, she typically handles the appointments and permission papers and becomes the IEP keeper. To effectively handle the child's requirements, cooperation is essential.

Finding assistance to prioritize requests, assigning some tasks to others, organizing papers, and setting up a timetable can all significantly improve productivity. A good organizer or behavior analyst can structure things like this for you and your loved one.

Putting Self-Care First

Parents who are overburdened may prioritize their own needs last. Stress and depression may result from this. This has the potential to make the situation very worse over time.

For all caregivers, self-care is essential. It's critical to understand that taking care of oneself is not being "selfish." Self-care, which is sometimes linked with spas and bubble baths, can entail attending to basic requirements like eating wholesome foods, getting adequate sleep and exercise, and spending time with family and friends.

In the long run, these activities enable parents to support one another and their children without getting worn out or overburdened.

Seeking Support

Special needs parents, in addition to feeling overwhelmed, may also feel lonely, ashamed, guilty, anxious, or depressed. Parents may process these emotions and begin to see the advantages of raising a child with special needs over time. In the meantime, support is available in a variety of ways, some of which are as follows:

- Local special needs parenting groups that meet in person.
- Online special needs parenting groups.
- Institutions like The Arc offer parenting programs and chances for connection.

- Life coaches or cognitive therapists who work one-on-one with parents to offer support and stress-reduction strategies. Ensure you find a healthcare professional who is familiar with parenting children with special needs.
- The Stanford University Autism Center at Packard Children's Hospital for parent training (PT) and remote Applied Behavior Analysis (ABA) resources.
- The National Respite Care Network for in home help.
- Behavior Analyst Certification Board (www.bacb.com) to find qualified Applied Behavior Analysis (ABA) and parent training (PT) services.
- Professional organizational companies such as A Clear Path to declutter and create harmony in the home environment.

Finding the ideal support system and modalities may take some time because every scenario is different. However, if we keep looking, we might find a "perfect match" out there for our own individual needs and circumstances.

Connect with Your Child

A lot of children with disabilities are nonverbal or have severe speech and social impairments. When this is the case, it may be challenging for parents to connect with their children. Given that it might be challenging to understand what your child needs, wants, or feels, this can be incredibly challenging.

Even the most basic of exchanges between parents and their child with special needs can enhance their relationship. Joint attention is a two-way street and there are ways to introduce this slowly over time. It benefits the giver and recipient through a mutual exchange of positive attention that is impactful on any relationship. We also found Positive Behavior Support and Pivotal Response Therapy (PRT) beneficial while we were trying to connect with Adam.

Finding joy

Parenting a child with special needs can, without question, be demanding, but it can also be a particularly joyous experience. Small victories can excite parents of children with special needs much more than they do parents of children who are typically developing. Celebrate those victories with your loved one along the way.

Children with special disabilities often have a particular awareness of and engagement with the world, which can be motivating. Parents are often able to recognize the delight that unique parenting can bring when they have the time and energy to see beyond the needs of the present. Making a big deal of even an attempt toward progress for your loved one will encourage them causing further gains. For example, Adam absolutely loved this when we clapped and said good job even at his slightest attempt to connect with us. Try this with your loved one for a very pleasant surprise in their response to you.

HOW CAN I HELP MY CHILD? WHERE DO I GO FROM HERE?

When we first start talking to people about the developmental and academic difficulties of our child, we often ask that question. It results from a sense of hopelessness. The variety of therapy alternatives seems too daunting to choose from because you have either exhausted all of your knowledge or are just starting your quest for understanding. The result is burnout or, even worse, a lack of ability to act. Parents are equipped to act quickly and confidently on behalf of their children when they are informed and supported.

It takes a village to help my child.

You shouldn't have to, and you can't, do this by yourself. Getting support for oneself is the best thing a parent can do when looking for help for their child. The ship is being steered by parents, and if the captain isn't operating with the best information possible, the entire crew suffers. Parents are advised to practice self-care, join support groups, use therapeutic services, and simply be kind to themselves. Give yourself a break, compliment yourself, and resist the urge to talk negatively to yourself.

Finding community and receiving support can be done in any way—right or wrong. Parents can get support in a variety of settings, including parent groups, one-on-one therapy sessions, yoga classes, and religious communities. Online clubs, blogs, podcasts, and books are all excellent resources. Instead of feeling lonely and alone, a parent might have a sense of belonging and connection by finding others with whom to discuss these subjects and share experiences.

Most parents picture mixing soccer games with ballet practice and grocery shopping when they consider the balancing challenge of raising a family.

But if you're a parent of a child with a disability or illness, your schedule probably also includes therapy sessions, doctor appointments, and waiting for insurance companies and providers to call you back.

Help is what you require. But how do you get it? Here are some suggestions for improving efficiency.

Accept the assistance of family and friends.

Everyone is busy, which makes it challenging to request or accept assistance. Because things might not be done the way you do them, it might be challenging to let the children or a partner help. Or maybe it's just not your style to tell folks when you're stressed out. After all, parents are expected to be adept at balancing everyone's demands and multitasking. You are not a superhuman, though. It is a show of strength, not weakness, to rely on others. Being reenergized occasionally can make you a better partner, parent, and person. So, go ahead and accept that friend or family member.

Tell the truth about your needs.

You're admitting others into your reality by telling them about your predicament. You provide a friend the opportunity to offer to go with you to the hospital by saying, "Going to the hospital by myself is hard." Your loved one understands that delivery of a warm meal will be very appreciated when you mention that it can be difficult to get dinner on the table occasionally.

List the things you need.

You've probably heard someone say, "Let me know if I can do anything," a number of times. And how many times have you promised "I will" and then broken your word? People want to help, but they are unsure of how. Write down anything that might make your life easier. After that, assign the task to the friend who will assist you the quickest. Need assistance picking up your other children from school? Ask a neighbor who is picking up their own children right now. Ask your grandparents and siblings to help with activities they enjoy, such as making meals that can be frozen or watching your child while you take a break. Utilize social media to make asking easier. Send out a request on your personal social media page or sign up on one of the several websites for caregivers. These websites allow you to indicate needs (such as weekly lawn mowing, companionship for hospital visits, or twice-weekly dinners), and friends can sign up for the jobs that best suit their availability and skill sets.

Invite more caregivers.

Parents with disabled children often believe they are the only ones capable of providing for their child's needs. But that doesn't exclude you from occasionally taking a short trip. You are teaching your child how to deal with change by leaving them with a dependable caregiver. Your child will acquire the adaptability and resilience that every child should learn.

Consider caregiver training to make sure the individual assisting you is capable. Siblings, parents, grandparents, instructors, and babysitters can take classes at a lot of hospitals and state social service organizations.

Consider home health care.

If your child has persistent or serious medical issues, you might find funding for the cost of an in-home health assistant or visiting nurse for a few hours each week. Check your eligibility by calling your insurance or government benefits provider. For children with impairments or developmental disorders, such as Autism, respite programs may also be available. A caregiver visiting your home to offer you a break for a few hours or an entire night, or a drop-off program in the neighborhood, are two examples of these services.

Consult experts.

Speak with a social worker who is part of your child's care team. Social workers can provide information about nearby programs and support that can lessen your load (and your bank account). This covers financial assistance, government subsidies, and respite care. You can get emotional support from social workers, and they can also show you how to find parent support resources. You can also learn about the resources by asking family advocates, such as parent advocates in your neighborhood Family Voices chapter.

Spend time with a friend.

Asking for help doesn't necessarily include making a request. Staying in touch with loved ones is often what a caregiver needs the most, and that can be challenging when your children need you nearby. So, invite a friend over once the children are in bed. Share a meal, talk over a pot of coffee, or watch a movie together. Spend some time laughing and interacting with people to relieve stress. In-person and online support groups can both be beneficial.

The majority of individuals really do want to assist. Your entire family will benefit if you let your friends, family, and care team know exactly what you need so they can help you shoulder the load.

2

NOTICING DIFFERENCES AND LEARNING TO COPE IN THE FIRST THREE YEARS

A genetic issue for Adam was revealed to us while I was pregnant, and the outcome was uncertain. However, terminating the pregnancy was not an option. I was already in love with my son. We knew the syndrome was not Down Syndrome, but we had a genetic translocation where information from one chromosome traded places with another that may or may not have been noticeable at birth.

At birth, Adam's Apgar score was a 9 of 10. Apgar is the score that assesses newborns one and five minutes after birth. The doctors said Adam was less than perfect because of an issue with his ears but I was relieved to see ten fingers and ten toes. When I heard there was an issue with his hearing, I knew he was deaf, but everyone said it might just be fluid in his ears. This is where my journey into special needs began. A mother always knows, and she keeps information close to her heart.

The world focused on Adam's Apgar score while I focused on him and how happy I was to see him born. He was, and still is, such a beautiful son. It was love at first sight and I was hopeful that Adam's genetic issue, a balanced translocation, might have been isolated to impact only his hearing. However, as an infant, I did notice differences in Adam versus other children.

Adam's balance seemed off and he did not sit up as easily. It was also hard to get his attention. However, that might have been related to his hearing. He had a lot of fluid in his ears but also in his nose and throat. Moving on to an ENT doctor, we discovered he had gastral intestinal reflux disorder (GURD). We also had the Audiologist perform a series hearing tests resulting in a recommendation to drain the fluid out of his ears. We hoped this would clear the hearing loss. However, to make a long story short, Adam was fitted for hearing aids at 6 months old. So here I was juggling multiple doctors within the first six months of Adam's life. And this was prior to his having been diagnosed with Autism. Special needs parenting can involve less severe occasions of special needs such as hearing loss or GURD.

Because of his hearing loss, the school contacted us to inform us of a government program called Early Start, which is part of the Individuals with Disability Education Act (IDEA) to provide early intervention in the life of a special needs infant in the hopes of maximizing possible gains for them. So off to the races I was as a special needs parent in the headlights. This resulted in my becoming aware of resources we could utilize in finding out if Adam's hearing condition was permanent or temporary. From there, we found that the hearing loss was permanent and then we had to determine if the condition was mild, moderate or severe.

At somewhere around 6 months of birth Adam was fitted for hearing aids and we started watching Signing Time videos to teach him American Sign Language (ASL), which could be used as a bridge to spoken language for all children. The first time Adam utilized his hearing aids, he smiled with delight as I sang him a song to give him his first experience at hearing my voice.

There is always a push of good experience with special needs that goes with the pull of disappointment of the diagnosis to begin with. It was just so rewarding to see Adam enjoying hearing the world around him. However, I knew I had to navigate the world of special needs as the school continued to test Adam for any other condition as part of IDEA to be sure he would get all the services he was entitled to. It was not until later that he was two that he was diagnosed with Autism. However, because of his hearing loss, we were on a fast track to early intervention for him.

As a result of our life experience, the planning challenges outlined in this book are from my personal experience. I hope these pages are helpful to parents as you navigate the life stages of your child with special needs with or without a formal diagnosis.

WHAT ARE SOME COMMON SIGNS THAT A CHILD HAS SPECIAL NEEDS?

Sometimes it will be obvious that your child has special needs. Other times, it won't be obvious.

The type and severity of any special needs or disabilities your child may have will play a role in this. For instance, a physical impairment like eyesight or deafness may be noticed right away. In contrast, modest learning disabilities like dyslexia or dysgraphia could be more difficult to spot.

You should find out as soon as you can if you think your child might have a special need. You can better understand the difficulties your child might have in the future with early detection.

Below are some of the warning signs and symptoms of various special education needs.

ADHD

There are nine behaviors that go along with the inattention symptom, which are listed below:

- Making careless mistakes or failing to pay close attention to details in school, the workplace, or other activities.
- Showing no sign of listening when addressed directly.
- Ignoring instructions and failing to complete homework, housework, or work-related responsibilities (not due to failure to understand instructions or oppositional behavior).
- Difficulty planning activities and tasks.
- Avoiding, detesting, or reluctance to perform tasks that need prolonged mental effort (such as schoolwork or homework).
- Being readily sidetracked by unimportant stimuli.

- Losing things needed for tasks or activities (such as toys, schoolwork, pencils, books, or tools).
- Being forgetful in daily activities.

The following behaviors are included for hyperactive and impulsive behavior symptoms:

- Leaving their seat in class or other settings when remaining seated is expected.
- Excessively moving around or climbing in places where it is not suitable. (in teenagers or adults, may be restricted to subjective feelings of restlessness).
- Fidgeting with their hands or feet or wriggling in their seat.
- Being "on the move" or often acting as though "propelled by a motor".
- Talking excessively.
- Blurting out answers before questions have been fully asked.
- Having trouble waiting for one's time.
- Intruding or interrupting others (e.g., butts into conversations or games).

If a child meets 6 of the nine requirements for the symptom of inattention, based on behavior over the previous six months, they may have predominantly inattentive ADHD. They may have ADHD that is mostly hyperactive if they meet six out of the nine criteria for hyperactivity and impulsivity. They may be given a combined ADHD diagnosis if they satisfy both requirements.

A family doctor or pediatrician can do an evaluation if a parent suspects their child has ADHD by reviewing the child's psychiatric and medical history and mental health issues and completing a physical exam. Additionally, to ascertain whether the child has ADHD, these specialists may conduct an interview with the parents and have them complete the Conners Comprehensive Behavior Rating Scale (Conners CBRS). Psychologists can conduct psychoeducational evaluations if a parent believes their child has a learning problem or another related disability. A student's cognitive capacity, areas of strength and weakness, any learning disabilities, and recommendations for additional support are all evaluated during these tests. A psychoeducational evaluation may also include a determination of a child's ADHD status.

Autism

Autism is often detectable or diagnoseable at a young age. There are numerous potential early signs of

Autism. The following is a succinct list of autistic symptoms:

- No babbling or pointing by the age of one.
- No single words after 16 months of age.
- No response when called by name.
- Poor eye contact.
- An excessive desire for quiet and order.
- A lack of smiling or social responsiveness.

Children with Autism who are toddlers or older may exhibit the following symptoms:

- Inability to relate to peers or make friends.
- Lack of conversational skills.
- Repetitive behavior.
- Repetitive or unusual language patterns.
- Preoccupation with things or topics of speech that resembles an obsession.

The list provided above is by no means exhaustive or official. These or other autism symptoms may appear to vary in degree because Autism is a spectrum disorder. Parents are advised to seek a medical professional's diagnosis if they see these symptoms in their child.

A comprehensive assessment, which includes a medical evaluation, medical and mental health history, and a speech and language assessment, can be performed by qualified professionals if a parent suspects their child may be on the autism spectrum. These professionals might include speech and language pathologists, audiologists, neurologists, psychologists, or pediatricians. To examine a child's communication skills, speech and language pathologists, in particular, can carry out speech and language assessments.

Language-based learning disabilities

The beginnings of a learning deficit based on phonemic awareness can be noticed in extremely young children. Problems with oral language are often warning signs. For instance, a kindergartener who has trouble rhyming should get special help. Children who have had trouble reading or writing in their families should also be properly watched. Oral language can predict a child's future success in reading and writing; pupils who have trouble pronouncing words or ordering word pieces may have trouble learning to read. Students with language-based learning impairments, for instance, might refer to an animal as an "aminal" or pronounce "bisghetti" in place of "spaghetti." Parents should keep a careful eye on their child's reading progress and shouldn't be afraid to question the teacher about what reading level the child is now at and how it compares to the standards for the grade.

Dyslexia

There are three typical symptoms of dyslexia in children.

- **Difficulty pronouncing and rhyming words:** Children of all abilities occasionally pronounce words incorrectly. However, parents should pay attention when a child experiences persistent difficulty understanding vowel sounds or switches syllables when saying a word, such as "butterfly," pronouncing it as "flutter-by." Additionally, young toddlers who may have dyslexia may find it difficult to recognize or rhyme even very basic words like "cat" and "bat."
- **Sluggish, inaccurate reading abilities:** Young children with dyslexia sometimes struggle to sound out unfamiliar words on their own, leading them to make assumptions about words based on context or to skip the word entirely. Parents may observe reluctance, hesitancy, or concern about reading in these

children because they take longer to develop their reading abilities.
- **Poor spelling abilities:** While its usual for all kids to mix up letters like "b" and "d" and other sounds, this confusion tends to go away sooner for typical readers and lasts longer for kids who might be dyslexic. Spelling is extremely tough for kids with dyslexia. Errors can be in many different forms, such as deleting a vowel or consonant letter, or a whole syllable while spelling.

I strongly advise parents who are worried about their child's reading not to take a "wait and see" approach because doing so can be extremely harmful in the long term and can squander crucial repair time. It would be foolish to waste time hoping that a reading impairment would magically go away because there is such a small window for a successful remediation. Parents shouldn't be afraid to request additional reading assistance at school or to hire a tutor who uses a method supported by research. A child may gain from a thorough psychoeducational assessment conducted by a licensed psychologist. The comprehensive and in-depth nature of these evaluations provides a very clear picture of a child's cognitive, learning, and socio-emotional profile.

Learning disabilities

When they believe their child is not learning as expected, parents often let teachers, or their pediatrician, know. There are indications that a child isn't learning to recognize letters, isn't interested in reading, isn't understanding what is being taught in class, has difficulties holding a pencil and writing numbers and letters, or isn't paying attention long enough to understand. This conversation might result in gatherings at the school where resource teachers and the teacher gather assessments and share suggestions. The teacher or pediatrician will advise a psychoeducational assessment with a psychologist if there are any concerns. Psychologists employed by school boards or privately may conduct this.

AFTER YOU FIND OUT THAT YOUR CHILD HAS A DISABILITY

Giving birth to a child with a disability or learning that a child has a disability can have a significant impact on the family. Here, we'll offer more details to assist the family's health, wellbeing, and life cycle when a member has a disability.

We are making this attempt to speculate about what might be in store for you and your family with the utmost humility. On the contrary, we want you to be as prepared as you can be to deal with any difficulties your family may face. On the other hand, we acknowledge that when a child has a disability, individual variety and variances are the norms. Researchers often base their conclusions on group data or what the vast majority of people experience in a situation. What might be "true" in the context of research, however, might not be true at all for your family. Therefore, while we hope that this section will guide you through the right path, only use what you need from our discussion.

The journey

Nobody wants their child to be ill, disabled, or in any other way harmed. Nobody anticipates having this experience; rather, it is an unforeseen journey. Families often have to go over tough terrain. Yet a lot of families are able to adapt to and manage the stress and problems that may come along with their child's illness or disability by drawing strength from within themselves and from their networks of support.

Many parents have discussed how their emotions changed over time after finding out that their child had a disability or impairment. Even though they may be strong and overpowering, the feelings that parents go through are normal and acceptable. Both the family and the individual experience a return to stability. Parents start looking for the information they need. Many people talk about experiencing personal progress that is often astounding to them looking back.

Together, the numerous recommendations and observations made by parents who have long dealt with disability in the family can offer parents who are just beginning the experience a lot of advice and support. This section will go through many of the ways Adam's father and I have assisted ourselves and those we care about in adjusting to having a child with special needs and providing for them.

Access to resources and services

This life stage for a special needs family involves collecting information on your child's impairment, the resources that are offered, and the precise steps you can take to support your child's development. The goal of these early years is to obtain a diagnosis and consider the treatment options for your loved one. This is the first thing you must do to enable your child and your family to map out a plan to move forward.

A crucial aspect of raising a child with special needs is gathering and utilizing the knowledge available about his or her diagnosis. Fortunately, there is a wealth of knowledge available on a wide range of disabilities and disability-related issues. Here are just a few of the resources that might be helpful at this life stage of your loved one.

Join a group

Parents just like you hold a lot of the knowledge that will be beneficial to you in their hands, minds, and hearts. It makes sense to join a parent group for this reason. Others bring together parents who, regardless of the disabilities of their children, share common worries, such as daycare, transportation, coping, or learning about and supporting special education in their community. Examples of the latter type of group include cerebral palsy, Tourette syndrome, and Down syndrome. Information, emotional and practical assistance, and common worries can all be exchanged within each of these groups. A common theme that runs across all of the literature published by and for parents is the ability of this mutual sharing to overcome emotions of loneliness, bewilderment, and stress.

Finding a parent group in your region can be done in a number of ways. Your state's PTI (Parent Training and Information Center) is a fantastic place to get started. The PTI may connect you with parent organizations both locally and statewide in addition to assisting you in understanding your child's rights, community services, and how to advocate for your child.

Reading parenting-related books is recommended

Reading many of the good materials on disability issues that are available, including books, articles, and websites, may also be helpful to you. Talking to your child's teacher, a local librarian, or another concerned professional can provide you with worthwhile recommendations for books to read, as can contacting a local, state, or national disability group or conversing with other parents of children with disabilities.

Learn about services

Families face a barrier in finding help because the needs of the child change with time. The majority of these services are made available as a result of federal and state laws.

Usually, cities, districts, and states offer a wide range of services to help you fulfill the requirements of your child with disabilities and your family. Early intervention services, which aim to identify and treat developmental issues as soon as possible, are recommended for families with young children with disabilities (birth through the third birthday). Special education and related services may play a significant role in meeting the educational needs of school-aged children with impairments.

Early intervention services: These services are created to meet the needs of newborns and young children with disabilities as soon as possible. These services might include everything from creating a comprehensive physical therapy program for a baby with cerebral palsy to providing feeding assistance from a dietitian in a hospital. These services are available to all children, not just those with special needs. Congress recognized the importance of families while drafting the law outlining early intervention services. As a result, while planning help for infants and toddlers with disabilities, the family's interests, concerns, and resources are taken into serious consideration. This procedure leads to the creation of a plan known as an Individualized Family Service Plan (IFSP).

Early intervention treatments are beneficial for both parents and children. They can learn skills that may be beneficial for a long time as full members of the team creating the program for their child, including skills in decision-making, planning, providing support to others, and influencing policymaking in their community.

They can also learn skills to help their child learn and develop.

The services themselves are provided in a variety of locations, including your home, a clinic, a neighborhood childcare facility or Early Start program, a hospital, or the area health department, and are supplied through a public or private agency. Your child's first evaluation and assessment will be free of charge. Although it may differ from state to state, services may also be offered free of charge. For services, some states impose a "sliding scale" cost.

Special services and education: Every qualified child with special needs is entitled to a free, adequate public education that is tailored to meet his or her specific needs thanks to the requirements of two federal laws, Section 504 of the Rehabilitation Act of 1973 and the Individuals with Disabilities Education Act (IDEA). A team, including the child's parents, plans this education.

The federal law known as the Individuals with Disabilities Education Act (IDEA) covers special education and related service programming for kids and teenagers with disabilities. When it was first passed in 1975, it was known as the Education of Handicapped Children Act. Amendments to the law were introduced in 1990, effectively renaming it IDEA. Additional amendments were made in 1997 and 2004 to provide equitable access to education.

This federal law aims to guarantee that children with disabilities get a Free Appropriate Public Education (FAPE) in the setting with the Least Restrictive Environment (LRE). IDEA does the following:

- Ensures that all children with disabilities are given special education and related services they require.
- Assures that children with disabilities are ready for independent living and the workforce.
- Ensures that families with children with disabilities have legal protection for their rights.
- Evaluates and monitor the efforts made by organizations that offer services to people with disabilities.
- Supports states, communities, federal organizations, and educational service organizations in their efforts to educate children with disabilities.

What is FAPE?

IDEA mandates that public schools offer a free, appropriate public education (FAPE) to all students with disabilities in the Least Restrictive Environment (LRE). As a result, schools must, to the greatest extent possible, integrate students with disabilities into regular classrooms with their peers without disabilities. FAPE is provided through an Individualized Education Program (IEP) that is tailored to the needs of the child in order to help them succeed in school and be ready for further education, employment, and independent living. IEPs include annual goals, progress monitoring, accommodations and modifications, related services like speech and occupational therapy, and more.

As a result, the team that decides what kind of special education your child will get includes you as parents as important members. The members of your child's team work together to create an Individualized Education Program (IEP), which outlines the educational plan for your child in writing.

Early Start Initiative

A one-year preventative intervention program called the Early Start Program is made available in a few schools in designated underprivileged communities.

The preschool program's goal is to combat educational disadvantage by focusing on young children who run the danger of not achieving their full potential in the educational system. The Department of Education oversees, finances, and evaluates the program.

In order to enroll, a child must be older than three years, two months, less than four years, and seven months on the first day of September in the enrollment year.

Either Early Start or the Early Childhood Care and Education (ECCE) Scheme is an option for enrolling children. Children cannot participate in both programs at the same time.

In 1994, the Early Start Pre-School Program was launched. On the Department of Education website, you may see a list of the schools that participate in the Early Start Program.

Early Start's objectives are to:

- Implement an educational program that will promote early children's general development and prevent school failure.
- Neutralize the impacts of social disadvantage.

Early Start aims to achieve the following goals:

- Children participating in the program will gain confidence in their capacity to learn.
- Children participating in the program will develop learning styles that are driven by motivated, organized and appropriately independent behavior.
- Children participating in the program will develop their language, cognition, and social/personal skills to the extent that they will be able to adapt easily to school life in the future.
- That the 'learning through play approach used in the program will be positive and enjoyable for the children involved.
- That the parents of participating children will become actively involved in their children's education.

DISCUSSING YOUR CHILD'S DISABILITY WITH THEM

It's crucial to discuss your child's disability, whether it be epilepsy, dyslexia, cerebral palsy, or another condition. You'll probably need to bring up the subject quite a bit.

Your child may have new questions or worries about their disability as they get older. Your response to these discussions will have a significant impact on how your child thinks about themselves and their potential.

Acknowledge the Disability of Your Child

Parents and guardians may, at times, want to avoid talking about a child's condition. They worry that bringing up the matter will make their child feel horrible or will make them believe they are not capable of succeeding.

However, avoiding the subject eventually does children a big harm. If a child doesn't know they have Autism, they cannot comprehend why they have trouble making friends. They could form false impressions of themselves and start to feel unlikable.

Similarly, a child who is unaware that they have a learning issue may believe they are not brilliant. However, they could feel glad to find that their difficulties are the result of a learning disability that makes them learn a little bit differently than most of their peers. Recognize your child's disability and be opened to discuss it.

Time is Critical

Disabilities come in a variety of forms, including sensory, intellectual, emotional, and physical. How you approach the topic will be greatly influenced by the type of disability your child has.

Your interactions with your child will also depend on when you both first learned about their disability. Your experience would be very different if you learned about your child's disability the day they were born when compared to parents and guardians who hear about it when they are ten years old.

Your attitude toward your child's disability will have an impact on how they see themselves, so it's critical to convey that they are capable children with a lot to contribute to society while simultaneously acknowledging the challenges they experience.

Be direct and honest in your communication

Your child's feelings will be impacted if you speak with too much emotion. If you express sadness over obstacles in their lives or worry about the future, your child might feel those emotions as well.

Give a straightforward explanation of your child's disability. Discuss the research underlying your child's disability or admit that while other children can use the stairs, your child needs an elevator. Don't offer too many opinions regarding those matters, though.

Avoid prolonged speeches and rambling inspirational lectures. Instead of listening to what you say, your child will observe your actions to understand more about their capabilities and potential in the future.

Be sincere while keeping the information age appropriate

Be truthful with your child when they ask questions about their health or outlook. Just be careful to present facts in a way that is child friendly.

When a 4-year-old ask questions about their hereditary problem, the neurobiology underlying their disability won't make sense to them, and a 10-year-old doesn't need to be informed of all the most recent medical findings in order to grasp why they take a certain drug.

Give your children clear answers to their questions. They will either ask more questions or rephrase an existing question if they need more information.

Simple expressions are, "Your muscles struggle to work with your bones," or "This medication helps your lungs function better."

Invite Your Child to Ask Questions

The questions that your child has regarding their disability will evolve over time. They'll probably have fresh questions as they reach puberty or when they start considering their alternatives for a profession.

Make it clear that you are always pleased to answer questions, and let your child know that they are welcome to ask questions of other people as well, such as their doctor or other members of their treatment team. Help your child in locating reliable people who will be receptive to their questions.

Discuss the individuals assisting your child

Talk about all the people who are working hard to support your child instead of all the ways they need care due to their condition. Describe the methods used by researchers to study the condition and the results they hope to find.

Additionally, discuss the commitment made by their doctors, therapists, instructors, and coaches to assisting them in realizing their full potential. Remind them that they have a large team of supporters that are behind their efforts.

Educate your child on appropriate things to say to others

It's possible that individuals in the community or other students at school will ask questions about your child's condition. While your child is under no need to give an explanation, helping them write a script for answering questions might make them feel more at ease if they decide to do so.

Find out from your child what they want the public to know. A child who is able to declare, "I have Tourette Syndrome, and that's why I twitch sometimes," may be able to stop a bully in their tracks. They could also be able to stop the rumors others are spreading about them.

With your assistance, have them practice it and then discuss how it goes when they apply it to others.

Pay attention to your child's strengths

Discuss your child's strengths with them. Let them know they are a skilled artist or mathematician.

Make sure children understand that having a disability need not prevent them from achieving academic success. A little more assistance can be all they need to accomplish their objectives.

Talk about all their strengths and affirm all the qualities you admire in them. It is much more likely that a child will feel competent and confident if they can identify their own abilities and skills.

Choose Positive Role Models for Your Child

Every child gets upset and discouraged occasionally. These emotions, however, can become widespread in children with disabilities. Finding positive role models who share a disability with your child can encourage them.

If there are professional sports, singers, actresses, or businesspeople who have a comparable condition, introduce them to your child and tell them about their accomplishments. If you are aware of a community adult who shares the same disability as your child, politely ask them whether they would be open to meeting with you both. A disabled child's life can be drastically changed by encountering and engaging with adults who have comparable life experiences to them.

Planning Considerations

Take notice here that planning here is centered around diagnosis and treatment planning in response to your loved one's diagnosis. Planning for the care and support for your child with special needs is the primary focus. Finding the right caregivers and the right treatment plan will have a long-term impact on the outcome and the earlier you start with intervention the better.

Enabling your loved one to be healthy and safe is the first priority. For this reason, many parents are focused on these aspects of planning beyond financial and estate matters at this life stage. Financial matters are more focused on cash flow and budgets in light of employment status of parents and funding. resources.

With regard to planning, the best help to parents is to provide a detailed understanding of government benefits in your state for special needs parents and the specific diagnosis their loved one is challenged with. Guiding families to advocacy resources is another way to add value. Being knowledgeable with relevant information and resource referrals is the best advise that can be offered.

Other aspects of planning will come into play once the treatment plan, home environment, and educational planning is initiated and implemented as they evolve and change over time. This is a lifetime planning challenge but over time, hopefully, less time consuming.

3

GAINING CONFIDENCE IN PRESCHOOL AND EARLY ELEMENTARY

All of us require confidence to truly succeed, but it can occasionally be more difficult for children with special needs to recognize their own value and worth. Your child may feel less secure and as if they are not truly understood by other children who don't have any restrictions or disabilities.

Regarding your child's confidence levels, you don't have to remain passive. There are things you can do right away to boost their self-assurance and your relationship with them.

BUILDING CONFIDENCE IN A CHILD WITH SPECIAL NEEDS

For children with special needs, it might be more difficult to establish value and self-worth than for other children. However, confidence goes a long way in defining who we are and how we act toward other people in our daily lives. The gap between reality and what is perceived as "normal" might widen as a result of disabilities and restrictions, separating children with special needs from other children owing to a lack of understanding. Is it just? No, everyone should have equal access to the necessities of life. Can we change it? Yes!

A child with special needs sees the world differently than typically developing children, which can lead to frustration and anxiety when they become aware of their limitations or don't get the outcomes they desire. This may cause a child to act out in a negative way or develop low self-esteem. Children who are repeatedly made to play by our rules either become discouraged or adopt an "I can't" attitude, which is understandable.

The technical term for the "I can't " attitude is "learned helplessness". To mitigate this tendency, I encourage improved communication and confidence in your child with special needs at this life stage. A child with special needs often excel in some areas to compensate for areas of deficiency. The skills they develop are often called "splinter skills". We need to follow their lead and work from their strengths in order to encourage them to benefit from their treatment and education plans.

1. Spend quality time with your child.

You spend every day with your child, so it can sound like a no-brainer. How can you not spend time with them? Spending time with them, on the one hand, fosters confidence in countless ways. Being around them, on the other hand, is different from spending time with them. By doing activities one-on-one with your child, you may demonstrate to them how important their world is. They will know you care about them no matter what by your complete focus on their interests.

It is important to stay engaged while also allowing your child with special needs time to be independent and engaged with other individuals. This is a dance that is difficult at first and that can be underutilized or overutilized at first.

In the underutilized scenario, it is possible to give a caregiver too much leeway causing your child to feel disconnected from you as his or her loving caregiver. This can cause an escalation in behaviors as the child acts out in attention seeking behaviors. It is possible that your loved one is cared for, but they might need to be further engaged or supported by you personally. Attention seeking behaviors are a sign that your child might need a slower transition into independence with more of your help.

The opposite can be true in an underutilized scenario when it is often mom who does too much and steps in causing a lack of interaction or engagement with caregivers. I have seen too many parents get burned out due to lack of their loved one's ability to accept anyone else. This presents a huge problem in later life stages. To avoid overdependence on you later in life, it is highly desirable to let your loved one work out relational difficulties with a therapist or caregiver while he or she is working on independence.

It is very important at this stage of life for your loved one to learn independence and interaction with other people. Instead of stepping in too often, implement routines and activities that could easily be generalized to a caregiver. This will pay dividends later in life as you age, and child becomes an adult who might be more difficult to control.

This is a perfect example of early intervention. Attributes such as independence can be taught early in life at a time when the brain is soft and your loved one is receptive to learning new things. Everything is new at this life stage and it is important to establish good habits that will last a lifetime. Making gains later in life is highly challenging and it is wise to start before your child is set in his or her ways.

2. Make use of encouragement.

Positive messages are more effective in influencing children and most people in general than negative ones. The "feel good" hormones dopamine and oxytocin are released in large quantities when we receive an encouraging message about our behavior. Things that make us feel good have a visceral reaction in our bodies, and we crave more of them. A child with special needs will feel empowered to accomplish more than they could have ever imagined if they continually hear encouraging words and positive reinforcement.

When you and your child are enjoying time together, you can give each other a slap on the back, a quick hug, or a big smile as positive reinforcement. You'll quickly notice a difference in attitude and confidence if you encourage them to feel good about their skills and recognize their efforts.

This is the essence of Positive Behavior Support, a behavioral therapy modality (method of implementation). If your behavior therapy at home utilizes this modality, it is possible to request Positive Behavior Support at school also. There must be consistency across environments as part of IDEA.

Since parents are part of the team at school, it is up to them to provide this type of collaboration to support their loved one at school. Otherwise, traditional discipline methods are utilized, which might confuse your loved one. In addition, caregivers and therapists are part of the team and they should be utilizing Positive Behavior Support in their environments also.

3. Discover activities that your child enjoys.

Nothing is more annoying than being made to perform an activity we repeatedly detest, especially if we aren't very good at it. However, it might be necessary for your child to learn non preferred behaviors. Behavior therapists and the educational placement have skilled workers who know how to utilize reinforcers to encourage your child to engage in non-preferred activities when making "demands" on them. Without the right protocols, however, simple tasks might turn into a nightmare for a child with special needs. This stresses the importance of having the right support for your child.

One red flag is if your child engages in negative or maladaptive behaviors who might feel frustrated more quickly than other children with certain people. This might trigger the need to evaluate the accommodations for your child and advocate for them. Investigate the antecedents to such behaviors to identify what functions they might be serving. Is your child engaging in avoidance behaviors or is he or she attention seeking? These are the questions you and the team should be asking to tease out what is going on when your child does not seem to enjoy what he or she is engaged in during the day.

In between "demands, folding in activities they like to do will make your child feel strong and validated. Does your child enjoy drawing? Sit down with them and color the images they draw for you, complimenting them on their work as you go. Are you able to calm your child down using music? Play the songs on your child's playlist while you listen together and compliment their taste in music. By including your child in things, they enjoy, you may show them that they aren't irrelevant to the rest of the world and that their preferences and interests are, in fact, important.

4. Give them a few modest responsibilities.

Giving your child with special needs a task, you are confident they can easily finish helps to boost their self-confidence. This can be done at home at first and then "generalized across environments". They will be able to appreciate their achievements and feel a sense of pride in a job well done, giving them the opportunity to utilize positive reinforcement. Your child may smile in agreement when you congratulate them with phrases like "Great job!" or "Way to go!" Just keep in mind to keep the tasks within their capabilities to prevent unwarranted aggravation and anxiety that can result from them being unable to finish the duty without parental support.

5. Take part in celebrations of their special needs.

Finding activities, they enjoy doing while honoring their special needs helps a child feel good about their accomplishments, much like little duties and individualized attention. Finding other children with the same limitations can offer a safe, regulated setting where your child can feel like just another member of the group. Outside support groups for children with disabilities know exactly what your child needs to develop confidence. Peer acceptance can significantly contribute to sentiments of self-worth. See if your neighborhood family support office can steer you toward a group your child may join or even involvement in your neighborhood community.

The encouraging message that you believe in their ability and want to see them succeed is reinforced when you concentrate on a child's strengths rather than focusing on what they are unable to perform. Giving children the support they require to develop basic skills boosts their sense of self-worth, self-esteem, confidence, and appreciation for their own strengths. And who doesn't occasionally need a good helping of encouragement in their life?

HELPING YOUR CHILD THROUGH PRESCHOOL AND EARLY ELEMENTARY

After the first three years of his life, we moved Adam from Early Start preschool years to understanding his rights under IDEA as he became eligible for elementary school. There was a shift from an Individualized Family Service Plan (IFSP) to an Individualized Education Plan (IEP) for his educational setting. This involved understating his individual needs as per his individual diagnosis. It also included implementing his chosen modalities as part of his treatment plan across multiple environments. Multiple environments including at home, in school, after school, and socially.

In the prior life stage, Adam was diagnosed with Autism after he was born deaf. Before the Autism diagnosis, he also had digestive issues related to Acid Reflux. Through the book "Special Diets for Special Kids," we decided to try a gluten-free/casein-free (GF/CF) diet. Then when Adam was diagnosed with Autism, we discovered the GF/CF diet could improve behavioral issues for Adam. So, because they overlapped with two of Adam's diagnoses, the whole family went GF/CF, and we all lost weight and gained energy. Helping Adam was actually helping us to the extent we were willing to follow his lead.

In this life stage, we began selecting protocols for Adam. There are multiple ways to respond to Autism, for example. These ways of treating a condition are called modalities. As part of IDEA, parents are entitled to determine the modalities that will be required of their child with the consistency of application (fidelity) across environments. As part of the planning process, it is absolutely mandatory to understand this. Some modalities are more difficult to implement than others, and this early stage of diagnosis includes advocating for the implementation of your child's modalities in all settings, including educational settings.

The Stanford University Autism Center was impactful in helping me at this stage with parent training as well as books and resources I could look into that were evidence-based and impactful. This is where I was introduced to Positive Behavior Support and Pivotal Response Treatment (PRT) as an applied behavior analysis protocol.

In our case, we also learned that American Sign Language (ASL) was impactful for Autism as a bridge for spoken language. ASL is also the language spoken in adult deaf communities. If Adam were to one day become a typical deaf person, learning ASL would be a chosen modality for him. However, the school wanted to place him in an autism classroom where he would need a 1:1 aid and interpreter. Thank God his father is an attorney because, at this stage, we discovered that advocating for your child includes understanding their rights under the law as well as resolving disagreements with the school district with regard to their recommended placement for your child, including accommodations.

The most crucial thing to do for a child with special needs is educational planning which includes placement and accommodations. Your loved one's ability to gain from his or her educational location must be validated. If not, it should be thought about making one or the other adjustment. To maximize results and avoid confusion, consistency across environments is also essential. The No Child Left Behind Act (NCLB) offers you a number of chances, so you should seize them and get through the challenges it presents.

NO CHILD LEFT BEHIND

IDEA and NCLB (the No Child Left Behind Act) are two of the nation's most significant federal laws pertaining to children's education. While IDEA places a greater emphasis on the individual child and strives to ensure that children with disabilities receive specific services so they can benefit from school, NCLB focuses on improving education for all students, with a particular emphasis on those from low-income households.

These two statutes have recently become more significant to parents of students with disabilities. All students must comply with NCLB requirements, including those who need special education. Parents should therefore be aware of NCLB's obligations. IDEA has been more tightly integrated with NCLB since Congress' most recent amendment, so it's crucial that parents understand how the two laws can cooperate to raise the academic attainment of students with disabilities.

What does the No Child Left Behind Act mean?

ESES (the Elementary and Secondary Education Act), the primary federal legislation governing education in the United States for students in pre-kindergarten through high school, was updated in 2010 with the passage of the No Child Left Behind Act (NCLB). As part of the nation's fight against poverty, Congress originally approved the ESEA in 1965. The primary goal of the ESEA, Title I, was to raise student success among the nation's poor and underprivileged students.

Some of the most important changes to the American educational system in decades were brought about when NCLB was enacted into law in 2002. In order to raise the accomplishment of all students, especially those with the lowest achievement levels, new standards implemented in NCLB were designed to improve the quality and efficacy of not only the Title I program but of the whole elementary and secondary education system.

NCLB is built on four basic principles:

- Accountability for outcomes.
- A focus on implementing strategies based on scientific research.
- More parental engagement and choice.

- Greater local flexibility and control.

By building on the standards-based reform initiatives put in place under the previous version of ESEA, NCLB seeks to:

- Raise academic achievement for all students.
- Bridge the success gap between groups of students who have historically performed poorly and their higher-performing peers.

Programs under Title I benefit 16.5 million students. All states currently receive Title I funding. In addition, a Title I grant is accepted by almost all school districts and 55% of all public schools. In 2006, the federal government provided about $13 billion for Title I programs.

What every state needs to do

By 2014, all states that accept Title I funding must have ensured that all students are proficient in reading and math. To accomplish that, each state must:

- Create rigorous academic standards that are the same for all students.

- Create annual academic evaluations for all students.
- Confirm that there is a highly qualified teacher in every classroom.
- Specify the amount of academic progress that school districts and schools must make each year to reach the proficiency goal by 2014.
- Ensure that at least 95% of students are tested in schools and school districts.
- Based on technical concerns, determine the minimal number of students that must be in required subgroups for yearly progress calculations.
- Ensure that reasonable adaptations and accommodations are available for students with disabilities.
- Create an annual performance report for the entire state and make it available to the public.

The accountability component of NCLB is centered on yearly statewide assessments (or examinations) of student progress. The results of these examinations, together with other crucial indicators, are used to assess whether schools and school districts make Adequate Yearly Progress (AYP).

Every aspect of NCLB is intended to hold schools, school districts, and states responsible for the academic progress of their students. Schools are judged on how well children are learning the knowledge and abilities prescribed by the content standards by requiring that all students in the required grades take part in examinations of reading/language arts and arithmetic. The ratings of schools are based on how well these specific groups of children are learning, not merely the performance of the entire student body, thanks to the need that the performance of specified groups of students (subgroups) be recorded. With this strategy, schools are held responsible for all students' learning.

Nothing in NCLB encourages or even requires states to link student performance on extensive exams to high-stakes sanctions. At the state or local level, usually by state legislatures, state boards of education, or local school boards, policies to make high-stakes decisions based on a student's performance on a state or district-wide assessment (such as being promoted to the next grade or receiving a standard diploma) are made.

Annual evaluations

IDEA mandates that students with disabilities must partake in all state assessments. IDEA mandates that children with disabilities take part in assessments if a state offers one that is more extensive than what is called for by NCLB.

Every state is required under NCLB to implement annual tests in math, reading, and language arts in grades 3 through 8, as well as at least once in grades 10 - 12. Beginning in 2008, science assessments also became necessary. The assessments must be in line with the high state academic content standards and be based on the state's established academic achievement standards.

Outcomes of this testing must be reported for the entire school as well as broken down, or disaggregated, by particular student groups that have a history of academic underperformance. These teams are referred to as subgroups. Performance information about each student is included in each grouping that applies.

Only when the number of students in a subgroup meets or exceeds the state-mandated minimum is the performance of that subgroup reported. Each subgroup's minimum size varies significantly between states. The following groupings are expected to be reported:

- Students from significant racial/ethnic groups
- Students who are economically disadvantaged
- English language learners

- IDEA-eligible individuals with disabilities – such students must each have an IEP in place each year.

The outcomes of the testing, along with other indicators like attendance and graduation rates, are used to assess whether schools are meeting AYP and making a significant and sustained increase in the academic attainment of their children. According to NCLB, the majority of children with disabilities are anticipated to take the same exams as regular students. A braille edition, additional breaks, or reading the math test may be modifications that some people require. However, the academic material being tested and the required level of achievement is the same as for all other children.

Students with disabilities have a variety of choices for participating in the normal exams, which are the same exams that all students take.

Routine grade-level evaluation

Most likely, a large number of children with disabilities will take either the standard grade-level state assessment or the standard grade-level state assessment with accommodations.

Accommodations for students with disabilities

States are required to make the necessary adjustments so that students with disabilities can participate in the full district- and state-wide exams. By leveling the playing field, accommodations ensure that the test evaluates a student's knowledge and abilities rather than the impact of their disabilities.

To ensure that students only use accommodations that result in a score that is legitimate for school accountability purposes, IDEA mandates every state to set rules for accommodations. For instance, reading the test aloud to the children as an accommodation would result in an unacceptable score on the test because the accommodation would affect the skill being tested, which is what the reading assessment is designed to do. However, reading the test aloud can be an acceptable accommodation if the necessary ability is text comprehension.

To the greatest extent practicable, accommodations used in state-wide and district-wide assessments should correspond to those used in regular classroom instruction and exams. Never introduce an accommodation for the first time in a state assessment. The IEP team for the child must decide which accommodations are required for state exams. The student's IEP must include a detailed list of these accommodations.

The following categories are used to classify accommodations:

- Presentation: (e.g., repeating instructions, reading aloud, using larger answer bubbles)
- Response: (e.g., mark answers in a book, use reference aids, points, use of a computer)
- Timing and Scheduling: (e.g., extended time, frequent breaks)
- Situation: (e.g., study carrel, special lighting, separate room)

Planning Considerations

Educational planning and treatment planning dominate the stage at this life stage for special needs families. This is the life stage that presents a challenge for parents because they are not familiar with their rights and the rights of their child. At this stage the best advice for them is related to care management as well as IDEA and accommodations they might be entitled to.

Rushing on to other subjects related to gathering assets might not be welcome at this life stage for special needs families. Instead, educational placement options and other possible areas of support for should be considered. In addition, evaluations should be considered because there might be a need for second opinions.

At this stage, parents are tapped out having to question everything in their hopes to enable their child to benefit from the services from his or her services. As progress is evaluated, shifts in placement or services might be implemented. Parents and the team of professionals working with them must be familiar with special needs planning topics as they think on their feet in response to their loved one's resource requirements for their development, care and support.

4

MAKING PROGRESS IN EARLY ELEMENTARY AND MIDDLE SCHOOL

As Adam continued to learn and grow, his intellectual abilities and communication improved. This meant he was able to learn more as we built on his gains. There was some confusion about what placement he should be in, the program for the deaf or a special classroom for special needs. The special needs classes did not use ASL, and this was his chosen modality, so we ultimately found a special school that utilized ASL that the district funded. However, this took quite a bit of work and advocacy for Adam.

The term "special education" covers a wide range of services that may be offered in various places and ways. A "one size fits all" strategy cannot be used in special education. The needs of a student with a disability are catered for in it.

Helping children with disabilities in learning is the main goal of special education. However, it doesn't entail keeping them in a specialized classroom all day. In fact, special education students are required by federal law to spend as much time as possible in regular classes. This is regarded as their Least Restrictive Environment (or **LRE**).

One student's services and support may be quite different from another student's in a variety of ways. Giving each child the tools they require to advance in their academics is the main focus.

Some students might, for instance, spend the majority of the day in a general education class. Others might only work with an expert for an hour or two in a resource room. Others might have to enroll in a different school that focuses on instructing students with learning disabilities.

Children with special education needs have an Individualized Education Plan (IEP). Their families are not charged for the specialized instruction or other assistance they receive. Specialists work with children on both their strengths and challenges. Families are important contributors to the team that determines what students need to succeed in school.

WHAT IS SPECIAL EDUCATION?

Many students are eligible for additional support and assistance in school. It is referred to as "special education." If a child's learning is hampered by a physical, cognitive, behavioral, or emotional problem, they may qualify for special education.

Special education ensures that all students who qualify get a free, adequate public education with their peers who are not disabled.

Examples of services may include:

- An Individualized Education Program (IEP).
- Speech therapy to assist with speaking, communicating, and feeding needs.
- Occupational therapy for assistance with daily tasks.
- Additional services and aids, such as a classroom aide.

Request an educational evaluation from your child's daycare or school if you are worried about their capacity to learn. The sooner children receive the necessary support, the better off they will be academically.

WHAT'S AN IEP?

Special education services may be available to students who require more assistance and support in the classroom in the form of an Individualized Education Program (IEP). This program describes the objectives and any support services that might be required for a child to succeed in school and is provided free of charge to families of children enrolled in public schools.

According to the Individuals with Disabilities Education Act (IDEA), parents and guardians of students with disabilities or special healthcare needs are crucial members of their child's educational team. They ought to collaborate with educators to create a strategy that supports students' academic success.

Your child will be more successful in school if they know how to access and use these programs.

Who needs an IEP?

An IEP is required for students who qualify for special education services. Students may qualify for a variety of reasons, but some typical requirements include the following:

- Autism
- Attention deficit hyperactivity disorder (ADHD)
- Cognitive challenges
- Emotional disorders
- Developmental delays
- Hearing problems
- Physical disabilities
- Learning problems
- Vision problems
- Speech or language impairment

How are services provided?

The majority of the time, the services and objectives listed in an IEP may be provided in a regular classroom setting. This can be carried out in a standard classroom. For example, a reading teacher helps a small group of children who need extra help while the other children in the class work with the regular teacher. The small group assists children who have comparable needs and are brought together for help.

Every effort is made to ensure that children with disabilities can learn alongside their peers who are not disabled. However, there are occasions when the required degree of support cannot be provided in a regular classroom. In these cases, children are taught in a specialized learning environment that is better suited to their requirements. Fewer students per teacher in these programs enable more one-on-one education. The teacher is typically qualified to assist children with special educational needs. Almost the whole day is spent in a small group setting, while they occasionally attend regular classes like exercise, the arts, or lunch.

WHAT'S THE REFERRAL AND EVALUATION PROCESS?

When a teacher, parent, or doctor suspects a child may be struggling in class, they contact the school psychologist or counselor, and this starts the referral process.

The first stage is to compile particular data regarding the student's development or academic issues. This can be accomplished by:

- A meeting with the parents.
- Meeting with the student to discuss performance.
- Observing the student in class to gauge performance (attention, behavior, work completion, tests, classwork, homework, etc.).

Officials at the school use this data to choose the best course of action. Sometimes all it takes to make a child more effective in class is a new approach. In the event that this is unsuccessful, the child will have an educational evaluation, which may identify a particular learning difficulty or other health issues.

It should be noted that disability in a child doesn't guarantee that child will get services. The disability must have an impact on the child's academic performance for eligibility. A group of specialists will evaluate a child's eligibility based on their observations, as well as the results of standardized exams and the child's performance on daily tasks, including tests, quizzes, classwork, and homework.

Who's on The Team?

You, as the child's guardian, can choose whether to have your child assessed. If you decide to proceed, you will be required to sign a permission form outlining the steps taken and the kinds of tests administered. These examinations could gauge a student's proficiency in academic subjects like reading and math or in developmental ones like speech and language.

Depending on the child's particular needs, the evaluation team may consist of any of the following professionals:

- A psychologist
- Classroom teachers
- A physical therapist
- A speech therapist
- A vision or hearing specialist
- An occupational therapist
- A special needs educator
- Others, depending on the child's specific needs

A thorough evaluation report is created once the team has completed the assessment. This report describes the child's skills and support needs as well as its educational categorization.

Before an IEP is created, you can study this report. To come up with a plan that best serves your child's requirements, collaborate with the team if there is anything you don't agree with.

HOW IS AN IEP DEVELOPED?

The IEP meeting, where you and the team will decide what will be in the IEP, is the next step. In order to provide advice on how the plan can help your child advance through the required curriculum, a regular teacher should also be present.

The team will examine your child's educational needs, as outlined in the evaluation report, at the meeting and create precise, quantifiable short-term and annual goals for each need. You can actively participate in creating the goals and choosing the areas or abilities that will receive the greatest focus.

The IEP's cover page lists the support services your child will receive and how often they will be given (for example, occupational therapy twice a week). Special education, speech therapy, occupational or physical therapy, counseling, and medical care like nursing or vision and hearing therapy are examples of support services.

Transportation, text help or changes, enrollment in special programs, and transition planning starting at the age of 14 are additional services that may be provided.

The amount of time they require in the child's academic calendar can appear overwhelming if the team suggests multiple services. A professional may consult with your child's teacher to develop ways that can lessen the workload but don't involve direct instruction. For instance, a classroom teacher may incorporate adjustments recommended by an occupational therapist into the handwriting lessons they teach their entire class for a student who has fine-motor issues that influence their handwriting.

Other services can be provided inside the classroom, preventing therapy from interfering with the child's day. While everyone else practices their handwriting, the child who struggles with it might work one-on-one with an occupational therapist. The child's comfort and dignity should come first when determining how and where services are provided.

Each year, you should evaluate your child's IEP to revise goals and confirm that they are receiving the necessary support. IEPs, however, can be modified whenever necessary and at any time. You can call a meeting and gather the team to discuss your concerns if you believe your child needs more, fewer, or different services.

WHAT ARE MY LEGAL RIGHTS?

Guidelines, sometimes known as procedural safeguards, describe your parental rights to influence what occurs to your child during the IEP process. Timelines, for instance, make sure that the creation of an IEP proceeds as swiftly as possible from referral to service delivery. Get a copy of your parental rights and inquire about this timeframe when your child is referred.

The parents' rights also outline your choices, including mediation and hearings, if you disagree with any aspect of the evaluation report or the IEP. Your local school district or early intervention services may be able to provide you with information regarding free or low-cost legal assistance.

If you require representation, lawyers and paid advocates who are knowledgeable about the IEP procedure will offer it. You may also ask anyone who knows your child or works with them and whose advice you think would be beneficial to the IEP team to join. Each state's federally funded programs promote parent-to-parent education and training initiatives for parents of a child with special needs. The Parent Training and Information Projects hold seminars, write newsletters, and respond to inquiries on parent-to-parent interactions by phone or mail.

WHAT ELSE DO I NEED TO KNOW?

Parents are entitled to decide where their children will attend school. This option includes public or private elementary schools and secondary schools, including religious institutions. Charter schools and home schools are also included in the mix of possible options.

However, parents should be aware that the rights of children with disabilities who are enrolled in public schools and private elementary and secondary schools are not the same as public education. There are two key distinctions that parents, teachers, school personnel, representatives of private schools, and students must be aware of:

- Children with disabilities who are enrolled in private schools by their parents may not receive the same services as they would in a public school.
- Not all children with disabilities enrolled in private schools will receive services.

Should parents decide to continue in a public educational setting, they continue to have input into the placement for their loved one as a member of the IEP team. However, they might need the help of an advocate if there is disagreement on the team as to the appropriate placement for their loved one.

Although the IEP process is complicated, it is a useful tool to address your child's learning style. Ask about the evaluation results or the goals the IEP team has suggested if you have any questions. You should take the lead in developing a learning strategy that is catered to your child's individual requirements because you know them best.

SPEECH-LANGUAGE THERAPY: WHAT IS IT?

Most children with speech and/or language disorders receive treatment through speech-language therapy.

What Are Speech Disorders?

An issue with making sounds is referred to as a speech disorder. Speech disorders include:

- **Articulation disorders:** These are issues with syllable sound production or inaccurate word pronunciation to the point where listeners are unable to grasp what is being spoken.
- **Fluency disorders:** These include issues like stuttering, where the flow of speech is

disrupted by odd stops, partial-word repetitions ("b-b-boy") or extending sounds and syllables (ssssssnake).
- **Voice abnormalities or resonance:** These are issues with the pitch, volume, or quality of the voice that cause listeners to lose focus on what is being spoken. A child with these disorders could experience pain or discomfort when speaking.

What Are Language Disorders?

A language disorder is characterized by difficulty comprehending or putting ideas into words. Language disorders may be either receptive or expressive:

- Receptive disorders are issues with language comprehension or processing.
- Expressive disorders include difficulties putting words together, little vocabulary, or a lack of socially acceptable language use.
- Cognitive-communication disorders include problems with communication skills that involve memory, attention, perception, organization, regulation, and problem-solving.

How Do Feeding Disorders Occur?

Eating or drinking disorder are referred to as dysphagia/oral feeding disorders. They consist of food refusal, coughing, gagging, and issues with chewing and swallowing.

Who Gives Speech-Language Therapy?

SLPs, often known as speech therapists, get training in the study of human communication, including its difficulties. SLPs evaluate a person's oral/feeding/swallowing, speech, language, cognitive communication, and other skills. They are able to do this and determine a problem's best course of action.

SLPs possess the following qualifications:

- At least a master's degree.
- State certification or license in the relevant profession.
- An American Speech-Language-Hearing Association (ASHA) certificate of clinical competency.

ASHA-certified SLPs have passed a national exam and finished supervised clinical fellowships that have been approved by the organization.

Speech assistance occasionally assists with providing speech-language services. They are often supervised by an SLP and hold a 2- or 4-year bachelor's degree.

Why Do SLPs Exist?

An SLP helps a child overcome issues in speech-language therapy by working with them one-on-one, in a small group, or in a classroom.

Therapists employ a range of techniques, such as:

- **Activities for language intervention:** The SLP will play and converse with the child while using images from books, objects, or current events to encourage language development. To improve language skills, the therapist could employ repetition exercises while also modeling appropriate vocabulary and grammar.
- **Articulation therapy:** During articulation, or sound production, exercises, the therapist will often use playtime to model the proper sounds and syllables in words and phrases for the child. The degree of play is in line with the child's developmental stage and demands. The SLP may demonstrate how to move the tongue to produce particular sounds, such as

the "r" sound, and will demonstrate how to make those sounds with the child.
- **Oral motor/feeding and swallowing therapy:** To fortify the muscles of the mouth for drinking, eating, and swallowing, the SLP may employ a variety of oral exercises, including facial massage and various tongue, lip, and jaw exercises. To improve a child's oral awareness during eating and swallowing, the SLP may also introduce various food textures and temperatures.

WHAT, YOUR CHILD MAY NEED SPEECH-LANGUAGE THERAPY?

Many conditions can necessitate speech-language treatment for children, including:

- Cognitive (intellectual, thinking) or other developmental delays
- Hearing impairments
- Weak oral muscles
- Cleft lip or cleft palate
- Chronic hoarseness
- Autism
- Articulation problems
- Motor planning problems

- Traumatic brain injury
- Fluency disorders
- Feeding and swallowing disorders
- Respiratory problems (breathing disorders)

The earliest possible tart to therapy is advised. Early therapy intervention—before the age of five—is associated with better outcomes for children than later intervention.

This is not to say that older children won't benefit from treatment. However, because they have ingrained tendencies that need to be broken, their progress can be slower.

What Role Do Parents Play?

The effectiveness of a child's progress in speech or language therapy depends heavily on the parents. The children whose parents participated in the program do so quickly and with the most enduring effects.

Ask the therapist for suggestions. For instance, you could assist your child in completing the SLP's recommended at-home activities. This guarantees the development and transfer of new skills. This is an example of collaboration across environments. Collaboration impacts your child's success due to consistency, or fidelity of implementation.

A speech or language problem might be difficult to recover from. Therefore, it's crucial that everyone in the family be patient and understanding with the child while they implement the same modalities across environments. This protects a child with special needs' gains while avoiding regression.

WHAT'S THE LAW?

Individuals with disabilities from birth to age 22 are guaranteed a free public education that is adapted to their needs, thanks to the Individuals with Disabilities Education Act (IDEA).

A plan that establishes learning objectives and incorporates accommodations (supports to aid in general education) and modifications (changes to general education) that foster achievement can be given to children who are eligible for additional support. The plan is developed in collaboration with parents, teachers, therapists, school psychologists, and others. Plans are available based on age and ability:

- **Individualized family service plan (IFSP):** Infants and toddlers up to age three who have developmental delays or medical disorders that can cause delays (such as being born early, hearing loss, or genetic conditions like Down syndrome) are provided with an individualized family service plan.
- **Individualized learning plan (IEP):** This describes a student's current academic standing and maps out doable learning objectives. If a student is 14 years old or older, it also contains how they plan to transition into life after high school, any adjustments or changes, and related services (such as counseling). A yearly review and quarterly progress reports are part of the IEP.

Where Do I Start?

Consult your physician. Inform your doctor if your child seems to be developing slowly or has special needs that make learning difficult. The physician can determine whether your child would benefit from an assessment or from seeing a specialist (like a speech therapist or psychologist).

Request or agree to an assessment. An evaluation will be requested for a child who may require further assistance to reach milestones. The early intervention program in your state or the neighborhood school system can help with this. Tests are used in evaluations to identify a child's strengths and challenges. Even without a prescription from your physician, you are welcome to obtain a free assessment. This is how:

- If your child is under three years old, contact the early intervention program in your state.
- Call your neighborhood school district if your child is three years old or older.
- You can always request an evaluation if your older child is having trouble in school. To schedule testing, speak with the teachers, the principal, a school guidance counselor, or a psychologist.

How Will My Child Be Tested?

The tests that are administered are determined by your concerns and your child's needs. Tests can evaluate a person's IQ, achievement, linguistic proficiency, motor abilities, development, and behavioral issues.

Which Services Are Available?

Infants and Toddlers

Infants and toddlers can enroll in the early intervention programs in their state. The majority of services, which include assistance with learning to walk, talk, play, and develop other abilities, are provided at home. Families and caregivers receive training on how to assist children in achieving their objectives as well as support in dealing with problematic behaviors or other issues.

Children are retested before they turn 3 to see whether they still require special education. If a child is eligible, a preschool enrollment strategy is established.

Preschoolers

Children typically receive assistance outside the home after the age of 3. Teachers assist in preparing preschoolers for kindergarten. Preschoolers learn best when surrounded by their classmates. This happens in preschools for special education or other learning facilities. A child may get additional treatments, such as speech therapy, if necessary, to assist in achieving learning objectives.

Children might have another evaluation after preschool is over to see whether they still require special education assistance in elementary school.

School-age children

Students from kindergarten age to age 22 may be eligible for an IEP or a 504 education plan, depending on their needs. A multidisciplinary committee must make the eligibility determination for students.

The 504 plan assists a child with a disability in succeeding in a regular classroom by providing behavioral and/or environmental accommodations, in contrast to the IEP, which specifies goals and offers special education services, including any adjustments.

Despite how similar the two plans may sound, a 504 plan and an IEP are not the same. A 504 plan changes a student's regular education curriculum in a regular classroom setting, which is the primary distinction. Teachers in the classroom keep an eye on a 504 plan. Depending on their needs, a student with an IEP may receive various educational services in a special or conventional school setting. The delivery and supervision of IEP programs are handled by additional school support employees.

A 504 plan does not require parental involvement or approval, although an IEP does. However, it's critical for the student's academic progress that parents participate fully in the 504-plan process.

It is possible to place students in a different school or program if their needs exceed what the school system can provide. Additionally, these students will need an IEP.

Teens

At the age of 14, the IEP will begin preparing a child for adulthood. We refer to this as "transition planning." The focus of transition planning is on the goals that a teen wishes to pursue after high schools, such as attending college or a technical institute, finding employment, or volunteering.

The young adult's potential residence and level of independence are also covered in the transition plan. It includes transitioning to adult health care services as well as life skills education (such as budgeting, travel, personal care, and domestic tasks).

When Do Plans Get Reviewed?

Every year, IEPs and 504 plans are evaluated. Every three years, there is a significant review that may need a re-evaluation.

Can I change my child's plan?

You can request a review at any time, as can anybody else on your child's planning team. If you have issues about your child's IEP, ask the IEP team to meet with you to address them. Guardians have the right to attend all IEP planning sessions, review student files, disagree with the plan, and/or request changes. IEPs are regarded as drafts until they are approved and signed by the IEP team.

You can engage with a mediator or file a "due process" complaint to help settle the difficulties between you and the school system if this attempt fails to provide the desired outcomes. You can also launch a lawsuit or make a complaint to your state's education authority.

While you go through the resolution process, your child will continue to receive services.

What Else Do I Need to Know?

It's possible that your child's path to learning is not the same as what you anticipated. Sometimes, the procedure could seem overwhelming. But remember that you don't have to go through it by yourself.

Seek help from the community and your school. Consult with other parents who have gone through the same thing. Participate in a support group, either in person or online.

Your child may learn and develop to their greatest potential with careful planning, patience, and cooperation from the school.

Planning Considerations

There is a lot going on and things can move quickly either for or against the needs for your loved one. This is your primary focus and you are tapped out with information overload. There is much to consider, and you are doing your best to learn what is required of your loved one to enable their growth and development.

This is a hectic life stage for parents and their loved one with special needs. This is the time when the individual needs of a child with special needs are revealed. The focus of planning advise is on the individual needs of a loved one with special needs. Time is of the essence to be responsive to those individual needs and create consistency across environments to avoid confusion, stagnation, or regression.

Planning continues to be primarily around care management and educational planning. However, the focus shifts from responding to a diagnosis to establishing a game plan from which modalities can be selected and implemented. Families are focused on evidence-based modalities and alternative therapeutic modalities that could be utilized and cost considerations are top of mind.

The best way to help families at this stage of their life path is to provide accurate and immediate information related to the resources they might have access to. Generic resources are related to personal assets and insurance coverage whereas non-generic resources are related to funded resources from the government. Experts in subjects such as these are welcomed. Giving their child the best possible means of success is of primary concern at this life stage for loved one.

5

SHINING BRIGHT IN MIDDLE AND HIGH SCHOOL

The goal of Adam's educational placement in elementary and middle school was to enable Adam to be included in the University High School regional program for the deaf (DHH Program). Because of our collaboration across environments and with the IEP team specifically, we implemented the same modalities for him at home and at school to maximize gains for him. This "fidelity of implementation" utilized evidence-based modalities for Adam to prevent regression.

The team worked well together to protect the gains Adam made in his earlier years hoping he would be included in the University High School's DHH program instead of the autism program at his home school with accommodations for his dual diagnosis. We believed inclusion with deaf peers and role models would benefit Adam. However, there were behavioral goals he must have mastered in order to be accepted.

In this life stage, we continued to work toward maximizing gains for Adam while protecting the growth of his levels of development. As a result, this life stage was primarily focused on Adam and assessments of his strengths and weaknesses. The effectiveness of protocols implemented were evaluated along with Adam's progress while we considered the evolution of his individual needs.

Educational placement, assessments, evaluations, and the development of coping skills were of top priority for Adam at this life stage. Ultimately, Adam was accepted to the DHH Program as a freshman in high school and he ultimately graduated from there. As a result of our earlier hard work and collaboration efforts, Adam enjoyed his least restrictive environment in High School. As a result, he was put in a position to learn from typical peers and role models using ASL as his primary method of communication.

We learned over these years that total communication is what has worked for Adam. This shifted in earlier years from the verbal behavior approach, to ASL as a bridge to verbal communication. Then we realized Adam was able to read lips, so we decided that spoken language paired with ASL was most impactful for him. Adam's entire treatment team collaborated and made modality shifts as we evolved with him.

The end goal was to maximize his potential and ultimately improve Adam's quality of life. And we are happy to report today that Adam was recently accepted to the Orange Coast College program for the deaf. I can now confidently say that my son, with the dual diagnosis by the age of two, gets to go to college. This is nothing short of a miracle and a testament to all of the angels and staff who contributed to Adam's success.

Aside from his educational and treatment plans in high school, we understood Adam would turn 18 in his senior year. Conservatorship needed to be considered so I could continue to manage his day-to-day activities. It is also at this life stage that we were required to contemplate government benefits (which are covered in the next chapter), supported decision-making, and self-determination for Adam.

CONSERVATORSHIP OR SUPPORTED DECISION-MAKING

Everyone has the power to make decisions, regardless of their support needs or level of disability. Various people make different decisions. Some people ask a few friends or family members for assistance in making decisions. Some people use gestures or actions rather than words to communicate their choices to others. But everyone has the power to make decisions, regardless of their support needs or level of disability.

The magic age of graduation for most people is 18 years old. And it is at 18 years old that guardianship or conservatorship is considered. There is an alternative to either of those called supported decision making that may or not work but that must be considered.

People with disabilities are often placed under guardianship because others believe they are incapable of making decisions. However, special needs individuals want to maintain their liberty to make their own decisions. Because people with disabilities can lose their autonomy when they are placed under guardianship, courts do require consideration of less restrictive options on or before a child reaches the age of 18.

As a legal status, supported decision making may not be possible to implement for some individuals.

However, there is a compromise. There are cases, like ours, that require active parental engagement in decisions for loved ones because of lack of comprehension in certain areas for loved ones. We engaged in supported decision-making strategies as an operating model for Adam throughout his lifetime. However, it was equally appropriate to seek limited conservatorship over him to manage his daily living requirements.

Limited conservatorship enables parents to make decisions concerning their loved one in the least restrictive environment at the age of 18. There is a more restrictive model, but it is not always granted. General conservatorship can give parents more control than limited conservatorship. However, it is costly due to legal fees and ongoing court accountings and oversight.

Since Adam did not own assets of his own at age 18, limited conservatorship was our first choice. Limited conservatorship was a means of defraying legal expenses. In addition, limited conservatorship enabled me to avoid court accountings and additional oversight. Ultimately, the court ruled that limited conservatorship was the least restrictive environment for Adam and we reserved a more restrictive environment for future consideration at a time when assets pass to Adam individually or in a special needs trust.

The concept of supported decision-making centers on the freedom to make decisions. The notion is that everyone occasionally requires guidance while making decisions. A person with special needs may require greater assistance. They could use a lot more assistance but needing help shouldn't be an excuse for restricting someone's options. Supported decision-making entails that a person can still make their own decisions even if they require assistance.

Some experts believe that supported decision-making should be used in place of guardianship or conservatorship. However, other experts disagree because of deficits an individual may display that might impact their decision making. There are practical details that need to be ironed out with regard to this model. However, it is important to be familiar with state legislation governing supported decision-making as you consider its merits.

HOW SUPPORTED DECISION-MAKING WORKS

In supported decision-making, a person with special needs receives assistance from persons referred to as supports when making decisions. Their friends, your family, or even your roommate could be their supporters. Their supporters won't decide for them. Every decision they make is their own. They just help. They might help you:

- Think about what you want to do.
- Understand the decision.
- Communicate what your decision is.
- Remember important things.

For instance:

- Wanda is an individual with autism. Wanda doesn't talk. She may point to images of objects she desires and then shake her head to say no. Wanda makes decisions with help.
- Wanda must employ a support worker.
- Her sister assists her in locating four candidates for the position.
- Wanda and her sister socialize with each supporter on occasion. Her sister records their responses to questions she poses to them about Wanda-relevant topics. Her sister asks Wanda about her impressions of each person after they depart. Wanda picks a photo that expresses her emotions.
- Wanda and her sister took a seat after all four visitors had left. Wanda's sister displays images of each person to her. She recollects Wanda's

feelings for each person. Wanda is reminded of the crucial questions that each person responds to.
- Wanda's sister calls the person in whose photo she chose to work with them to let them know that Wanda has decided to hire them.

Sometimes there is just one person standing by their side. There may occasionally be a few supporters. Or perhaps many people will occasionally support them. Making a decision on their level of support and naming supporter(s) is crucial. Additionally, they should be able to get rid of or change their supporters at any time.

Both significant and minor decisions can be made with supported decision-making. You can make use of supported decision-making for your loved one to choose what color shirt to wear. Using aided decision-making, they can decide if they want to have surgery. And so on.

The majority of people employ supported decision-making on a daily basis (not just used by people with special needs). For instance: A person would be using supported decision-making if they required an accountant to assist them in thinking through their finances.

They are assisted by the accountant. Their supporter is the accountant.

It is typical for all persons to require assistance with some decisions. However, the ability to make decisions with support is crucial for those with special needs. It aids in self-advocacy and the ability to make significant life decisions. However, your loved one must have the ability to comprehend decisions they are making and the implications of such decisions. This is often the subject of debate among professionals as to the practical application of supported decision making for certain individuals.

TYPES OF SUPPORTED DECISION-MAKING

The majority of supported decisions are made without you having to appear in court or fill out any paperwork. The benefit is you don't need to fill out paperwork to seek help from others in this model. Although forms are used in some processes, the critical form certifies that the government is aware of your usage of supported decision-making. This compares to conservatorships or guardianship where a judge rules over a determination as to the least restrictive environment and awards limited or general control over a conservatee to a conservator or guardian.

For people with special needs, doctors, banks, and other places they visit may require them to present proof as to which model they fall under. They must submit the supported decision-making form prior to making their own decision. The form may also specify that they are allowed to receive assistance from their supporter.

Each form for supported decision making performs a different function. Some of the forms are as follows:

Supported decision-making agreements

Written agreements that demonstrate the use of supported decision-making are known as supported decision-making agreements. You consent to receive advice on decisions from a person or group of individuals you trust when you enter into a supported decision-making agreement. These people are on your side. Their names appear on the form. According to the government, businesses are required by the state government in the form's jurisdiction to assist your supporters. Currently, only a few states use these forms.

Power of attorney form

A power of attorney document grants someone else the authority to handle financial matters or make legal decisions on your behalf. The word "attorney" is a term for "lawyer." But a lawyer is not required to make choices on your behalf. This power is revocable at any moment. If a judge rules that you are no longer able to make decisions, a power of attorney does not function unless it is a durable power of attorney. Even if a judge rules that you are no longer able to make decisions, this type of form still functions. These kinds exist in every state.

Health care power of attorney

A healthcare power of attorney is the same kind of document but one that deals solely with health care. If you become unable to make choices about your health care while you are ill, a healthcare power of attorney appoints someone else to do so. However, releasing the power of attorney while you are still ill can be challenging. These kinds exist in every state.

Healthcare advance directives

Healthcare advance directives specify your preferences for healthcare in advance in the event that you are unable to do so later. An advance directive for mental or physical health is possible. Advance directives for mental health are often known as "psychiatric advance directives." Doctors and hospitals typically are not required to follow your advance instruction, unlike a power of attorney. It merely clarifies what you want from them. These kinds exist in every state.

Authorized signatory form

You can fill out an authorized signatory form for a bank. The approved signer or authorized signatory is stated to have access to your bank account. They may also withdraw funds from your account. Be careful because this form gives your supporter access to your funds to manage and spend.

Additionally, you might configure your bank account so that both you and your supporter must consent before the money is withdrawn. By doing this, you can ensure that your supporter isn't using your funds secretly. However, it also implies that you must inform your supporter before making any purchases.

Additionally, you can ask the bank to set up a trust for you so that other people (known as trustees) can manage and save money for you so that you can only use it in the future. But you are limited in how you can use the funds. You might need to get authorization from the trust.

HOW TO SET UP SUPPORTED DECISION-MAKING FOR YOUR CHILD WITH SPECIAL NEEDS

Select the areas in which your child needs assistance. Examine the worksheet provided by the National Resource Center for Supported Decision-Making to identify the areas in which your loved one needs your assistance.

- Complete the supported decision-making agreement form. Sample agreements and forms are available at www.supporteddecisionmaking.org.
- Sign the contract in the presence of two witnesses, including a notary public, who attests to legal documents. No need for a lawyer or a court appearance.
- Distribute a copy of the agreement to any parties who will be impacted by it, including

your child's bank, school, doctors, and health insurance representative, as well as anyone else who needs to be informed that you are guiding your child's decisions.
- That agreement may be terminated at any time by you or your child by tearing it up and notifying the parties who received copies of it.

Additionally, you may need to ask your loved one to sign release paperwork if they require assistance with their health care or education.

Needless to say, many individuals with special needs might not have the capacity to understand and comprehend the data that is included in. the agreements and forms and this model assumes they have capacity to sign such agreements. The alternative is a traditional model such as a conservatorship or guardianship, depending on your loved one's individual needs.

HOW TO SUPPORT YOUR CHILD WITH DECISIONS AT ANY AGE

Even without a formal agreement, you can support your child's decision-making in day-to-day activities by using a supported decision-making strategy. And if you begin this when your child is still a young child, it can be easier to continue until they reach adulthood. This is what we have done with Adam. He feels fully empowered and engaged in decisions impacting him even though I have limited conservatorship over him.

You probably won't make important decisions in your life entirely by yourself. You most likely make a call to a friend, speak with your family, or seek another person you trust for advice. You then decide what to do.

A formal or informal supported decision-making process has three steps:

- Assist your child in obtaining the knowledge necessary to make a decision.
- Assist your child in considering all the implications of their decision.
- Assist them in communicating or cooperating with those who must be aware of their decision.

You don't have to make all decisions for your loved one while you support them. You can assist them in taking charge of their own decisions. Say, for instance, that your child has the opportunity to take both a dance class and an art class after school.

- Assist your child with information gathering: What is the cost of each course? When do the classes start? Is it possible to combine the two? How do they plan to get to and from the classes? Which friends might also be enrolled in the dancing or art class?
- Discuss it rationally with them: What about the art class do they like? What makes the dance class exciting? Will one of the classes keep them too busy or worn out to complete their other obligations, such as homework? How will they or you cover the cost of the courses? What do they anticipate learning or taking away from each class?
- Decide and communicate your choice. Your child may require assistance enrolling in the class or informing their peers about it after making their final choice. You can demonstrate to them how to call to register for the class, fill out the application on paper, or submit it online. You can assist them in keeping in mind to inform their friend that they will also be in the lesson if they are aware that their friend is enrolled. Some of these things might be necessary for you to do, depending on your child's age and skills.

Start small when they are young and work your way up to more complex decisions as your child matures and ages. In this way, you are preparing yourself and your loved one for the future as engaged individuals who are in control of their own life.

Additional Strategies to Support Decision-Making

Making decisions is not always simple. When you and your child must make significant decisions, the following tools may be useful:

- Your child can have a person-centered plan.
- A transition plan is a technique to assist you and your child in preparing for the decisions that will be presented to them as they enter adulthood.
- You can connect with other parents who are also striving to help their children make smart decisions as they grow up.
- Consider creating a personal network of other people who will commit to your child and help make sure they are well cared for.

There are various ways you might collaborate with your child to make smaller and larger life decisions because every child has different needs. You are still your child's parent even after they become 18 years old.

It can be easier for you and them to engage in a special needs planner or a Chartered Special Needs Consultant to prepare for the transition to adulthood. There are complexities involved that only a qualified expert can navigate. And these decisions are critical due to their impact on your loved one's financial future and quality of life.

SELF-DETERMINATION AND CHILDREN WITH SPECIAL NEEDS

The idea of self-determination holds that everyone has the right to live their lives to their satisfaction and to decide what will happen to them in the future. In most states, self-determination is also the way in which special needs consumers gain access to much needed resources.

All people should have the chance to learn and use self-determination skills, but young people with disabilities especially need these opportunities. Your loved one should be in control of their resources. With your help, and they should be in a position to utilize the support they are entitled to while also deciding on the vendors or individuals they interact with as part of their person-centered plan.

For information on your State's position on self-determination, check your State Council for Developmental Disabilities. In California, the first step in the process is to develop a person-centered plan based on your loved one's individual needs, then the Regional Center proposes a budget offer that may or may not be accepted. Then a spending plan is developed that is responsive to the person-centered plan, which can be revised if there is a change in circumstances. In California, there are independent facilitators who can assist with this process who can be found via www.thecasdpnetwork.org.

It is very important to note here that self-determination is different than supported decision making. Our responsibility as parents is often to safeguard our children and shield them from danger. However, we need to enable them to grow by fostering their independence.

By making their own decisions, our loved ones will be active participants in their own life feeling more validated and in control. This ability will pay off in the long run since, according to research, students with good self-determination abilities are more likely to succeed in the transition to adulthood, including finding a job and independence.

HOW ARE SKILLS IN SELF-DETERMINATION BUILT?

Children learn new abilities most effectively when they practice them and are certain that they will be encouraged if they make mistakes. It takes time to develop self-determination skills; it starts in childhood and lasts into adulthood. It's never too late to start if you're concerned that you haven't assisted your child in the development of these abilities. The "Tips for Families" section in this chapter provides detailed advice for fostering the development of these abilities.

Making judgments and exercising self-determination are taught abilities. Like any learned skill, this one might need to be broken down into smaller parts, with each step building on the previous one. Keep in mind that learning takes time. Both you and your child deserve your patience.

HOW CAN FAMILIES ENCOURAGE AND SUPPORT SELF-DETERMINATION?

Through support and exercise: Giving our children a chance to make their own decisions from an early age can help them develop self-determination. Allow your loved one make short-term decisions like what to wear or what to eat for a snack before moving on to longer-term choices like which classes to enroll in during their final years of school. Young children can gain from participating in gatherings where their accomplishments, successes, and skills are discussed, such as Individual Education Plan (IEP) sessions with school administrators.

When your loved one is prepared, you can work with their schools to include them in discussions about community, recreational, and employment opportunities. This will provide young adults with the knowledge and experiences needed to make their own decisions as adults.

Through Peer Mentoring: Connecting with people who have "lived it" effectively and grown more independent is a crucial step in assisting our children with disabilities in exploring their alternatives for the future. It's also referred to as peer mentoring. The staff at your child's school might be able to facilitate this relationship.

TIPS FOR FAMILY TO PROMOTE SELF DETERMINATION

What can families do to support and foster their children's capacity for self-determination? Here are some concepts to consider:

1. Model Expectations

- Show your child that you want them to be treated with the same respect and rights as children without special needs.
- Request that medical staff and other experts speak with your child directly.
- Expect that a child with a disability will lead a full life in the community.

2. Provide options

- Offer options for things like what to wear, what to eat, and what to do for fun or for family gatherings.
- Involve children in decisions about their education, health, and other matters in ways that are important to them.
- Inform your child in a way that is appropriate for them and give them time to respond.

3. Examine the possibilities of Options

- Encourage your child to regularly explore the neighborhood through outings, reading, and neighborhood activities.
- Discuss the future with your child in the same manner you would with any child who is typically growing.

4. Exercise self-awareness and self-advocacy

- Discuss your child's special needs or medical conditions with them.
- Encourage your child to discuss his or her special needs with others.
- Look for chances for your child to use self-advocacy and leadership abilities at school, in your place of worship, with friends, and through other initiatives or programs offered by the community.

5. Establish goal setting and planning processes

- Talk to your child about setting goals and making plans for future wants and needs. Give an example of how your family saved money

to buy a new item for the home.
- Use road maps or other image charts to help them visualize the actions necessary to accomplish their goals.

6. Acquire a tolerance for taking risks

- Consider ways to gradually and safely step outside of your comfort zone.
- List the risks that you would allow your child to take and weigh the advantages and drawbacks of each.
- Have patience with your child and with yourself. As with all people, these abilities can take time to develop.

In essence, the two ideas—supported decision-making and self-determination—share the goal of fostering young people's independence so they may participate in making decisions about the services and supports they receive. Supported decision-making ought to be the standard operating procedure for teenagers and adults with special needs. However, this does not necessarily mean that this should be the legal status of a disabled adult child. Conservatorship might be a practical avenue to explore.

Planning Considerations

There are important planning considerations at this life stage for your loved one with special needs. As needs change and evolve over time, flexibility is required in the planning process to allow for responsiveness to change. Strengths and weaknesses should be identified at this point of your child's life so that your loved one feels confident enough to take steps toward independence and graduation as he or she moves on to transition to adulthood.

It is important, however, at this life stage to start planning for the attainment of age 18. Is conservatorship needed? If so, will both or one of the parents seek conservatorship over their disabled adult child? Will supported decision making work instead of conservatorship? What about self-determination?

This life stage is where parents begin to engage legal experts to gain insight. Top of mind is the decision on the least restrictive environment for their loved one at the age of 18 and there are attorneys who are experts in probate court. Then parents continue to plan for the future beyond school years for their loved one with special needs.

It is at this stage when I also considered an expert evaluation of my estate plan to be sure I factored in all of the required special needs concepts for Adam. There were deficiencies in the original plan and revisions were made to meet Adam's individual needs as he entered into adulthood. This was an important step to take in that my estate might have ended up in probate court, even though I had established a living trust with special needs provisions in it for Adam.

Offering a review of the estate in light of special needs planning is a valuable level of support advisors can offer at this life stage. This is also the life stage when government benefits experts will add value. The definition of a disability is different for the social security administration than it was in the educational system and a qualified special needs expert can help you maximize utilization of government benefits.

6

A GENTLE TRANSITION FROM SCHOOL TO ADULTHOOD

What will happen to my loved one with special needs when I am gone? This is the question that comes to mind as I contemplate the future for Adam. I have done so much over the years for Adam and he has come so far. I often wonder what would happen to him when I am gone. But for now, let's focus on Adam's high school graduation experience.

After all this hard work and effort on the part of family and the IEP team, Adam graduated from high school on June 1, 2023 and we had grad night on June 2nd. The experience was epic, and I will take time here to bring to light how the life stages before this one did bear fruit for Adam. Doing the extra work early on is exactly what will benefit Adam for a lifetime, and it was well worth the effort. I hope you agree after reading this.

I found myself with mixed emotions as we went into the planning process for this incredible shift in life stages for Adam. At the same time as Adam's transition to adult services, I was shifting my work to build my own practice with fiduciaries including the special needs community in my career focus. So, this time was a huge shift for both of us. In addition, I was asked to present on the topic of this book at a conference for fiduciaries. The presentation timing overlapped with grad night and I had to decline the opportunity to share my knowledge with the membership.

I hope to host a session for Professional Fiduciaries of California (PFAC) on another day. However, for today, this was one of the sacrifices I had to make. For Adam, I needed to focus on this shift out of high school and make it fun for him. This meant that I need to be completely present for him as we celebrated in the graduation ceremony and for grad night. Needless to say, PFAC understood and we decided I would present on the topic of this book another day. I am actually glad it worked out this way because I will talk about this life stage and how rewarding it was when Adam graduated from high school.

Graduation date was exceptional. Adam was so excited, and I was very happy that I decided to focus 100% entirely on him and his experience shifting to this life stage. Adam had been accepted into the Orange Coast College Program for the deaf and we needed to implement programs for him at home and school so he would understand what would happen for him after high school. We did this so graduation would be a celebration and not just a goodbye.

Many children, and their parents, at this life stage are riddled with uncertainty for the future so it is important to map things out like this for them. In the exit IEP, we learned there will still be an IEP for Adam until he reaches the age of 22 when he "ages out" of educational services. The school had become so attached to him, they were sad to see him move on and that exit IEP was very emotional. Even his teacher was just too proud and emotional. The entire IEP team and I were amazed at how far Adam has come to grow into the beautiful young man he was in his suit, and cap & gown.

What was amazing for me to discover was that the Deaf and Hard of Hearing division of University High School in Irvine, CA created an inclusive experience for Adam at the ceremony. He received the appropriate behavior support at the ceremony, which meant he could fully participate. In other words, he was mainstreamed at school so he could fully participate with his typical peers and role models during the graduation ceremony.

Adam walked in with his class and sat down, with an attendant, in the seats with the rest of his class. He walked up on the stage and accepted his diploma and he walked off the stage with attention and grace. Everyone was so proud of him. The Orange County Register was there, and they took his picture and asked for his name. Furthermore, Adam sat through the hundreds of others who did the same and he tossed his cap with the rest of the class as the ceremony closed to congratulate the Class of 2023. It was a huge moment for Adam, the IEP team, and our family.

Adam understood he is going to college like many of his peers and he was able to close the chapter on high school without concern for his future. However, I was filled with uncertainty. I was talking to school and our in-home ABA vendor asking for a shift in our services. We needed to implement protocols for transition to adulthood and collaboration with the college placement needed to be initiated. We wanted to do what we did successfully with University High School in the transition program to maximize future and continued success for Adam.

PLANNING THE FUTURE FOR A SPECIAL NEEDS CHILD | 155

What will happen to my child when I am gone? This question was front and center for me again because Adam was now an adult with adult services and he only had about four years left of assistance from IEP resources. Thank God the principal of the Deaf and Hard of Hearing (DHH) program at Uni High, David Longo, is an expert in managing Adam and me. He took the lead with Adam as he closed the chapter of this life stage and opened the next one. The entire staff at the school was there and they were just so proud of Adam as he participated in his graduation ceremony.

Then off to grad night. We went to Disneyland with the rest of the class and I was a chaperone to be sure that Adam had a nice time. It was the best night of my life and Adam's. We got there early so Adam could do things I knew he would be rigid about with the class so he could get that out of his system. He was so excited watching the Ferris Wheel and eating popcorn when we got there, it looked as if he had taken a shower. By the time everyone else arrived, his sweat had dried, and his excitement levelled off (thank God).

Then, the other students arrived. We never caught up with the DHH classroom, but we enjoyed the sign language interpreters throughout the park that Uni High had arranged for. The DHH accommodations were spectacular and made Adam feel included. Then we reached out to a neurotypical friend of ours who Adam has known all his life and let her know Adam had a pass to quicken the line for rides if she wanted to join us. So, Adam had the most beautiful and p0pular girl in school at his side as he enjoyed the night that went all the way into the morning. He is very handsome himself and he is always popular at Disneyland.

Katrina, her two girlfriends, and Adam rode rides throughout the night and enjoyed a dance party just before boarding the bus back to the parking lot at 3:00 in the morning. Adam did not want to miss a minute of the experience and I was there to enjoy it with him while taking pictures that ultimately made the way into a video we posted the next day. Katrina said the night was magical for her also.

With the right support, Adam had the night of his life and you could see that in his face and in his behaviors. The glow from it all lasted for days and we have the pictures any time we want to revisit the memories. We were proud of Katrina also for wanting to hang out with Adam. They were born at the same hospital within months of each other, they experienced COVID together, and now they got to share this night together. I am beyond grateful and it warms my heart as I write this.

Back to this book. There was a woman who sat next to me before the park closed for grad night and she asked if she could ask me a question. It was while Adam and I were at the Ferris Wheel before the class of 2023 got there. She asked, how did you do it? She was there with her family and one of her children was on the spectrum. I shared a link to this book with her and it was no accident that, of all people, she would ask me that question.

My personal goal is to have many experiences like this with Adam hoping I outlive him by at least one day. But, for now, let's focus on this life stage and subjects outside of graduation to consider. The transition to adulthood shines a flashlight on the fact that your loved one is dependent on you as an adult. Subjects like conservatorship, guardianship, government benefits, and adult placement services are priorities at this life stage. Special needs planning and succession planning takes center stage as a result.

Although a certain level of estate planning has likely been accomplished in the prior life stages, there are other aspects of a special needs plan that need to be considered. For example, the subject of special needs trusts comes into play as family members pass assets to their beneficiaries. A special needs trust is a way to pass assets to your loved one with special needs while protecting government benefits. This is where the family might begin to engage special needs planning experts.

At this life stage, it is important to supplement the help of traditional advisors with special needs experts to avoid costly mistakes. There is an industry of special needs experts including lawyers, fiduciaries, financial advisors, special needs consultants, and so on who can be found via a simple google search. One resource is the Special Needs Alliance which can be found at www.specialneedsalliance.org.

Your loved one with special needs has different needs than your other beneficiaries. For example, protecting your loved one's entitlements, such as government benefits, must be a primary consideration in his or her estate and financial plans. Asset depletion analysis must also consider resources that are funded by insurance or government benefits and income from social security must be factored in. It is imperative to work with advisors who are experts in the protection of government benefits for special needs consumers.

A fiduciary who manages the affairs of a loved one with special needs is required to protect government benefits. Experts must attest to that fact as they administer your loved one's needs. There are other fiduciary standards of care that fiduciaries are held to so it is very important to engage advisors who will acknowledge this standard of care in writing. Otherwise, advisors might be simply bound to a best interest standard, which is not always to your advantage.

There are different types of fiduciaries. There are fiduciary financial advisors who can implement the Uniform Prudent Investor Act for your loved one to defray expenses and manage risk. There are also special needs fiduciaries who would be named as trustee over the assets of your loved one after you are gone. Alternatively, you would name a family member who would be considered a family fiduciary, but a fiduciary, nevertheless.

A professional fiduciary may come in at this stage of life for your loved one as a successor to you so you can begin to plan for the future. This is part of a well-balanced estate plan that would be established with a special needs planning attorney. This needs to be planned for in advance of needing them so they have an understanding of your loved one's needs before you are gone.

This is the life stage when you might take the time to create or update your estate and financial plan. Again, it is important to work with fiduciary financial advisors who understand the Uniform Prudent Investors Act to avoid financial exploitation of your loved one. There are many advisors who are interested in gathering assets, but few who fully understand the individual needs of a special needs consumer.

A GUIDE TO SPECIAL NEEDS GUARDIANSHIP: WHEN YOUR CHILD REQUIRES ADDITIONAL LEVELS OF SUPPORT

As previously discussed, when a person reaches the age of 18, they are considered an adult and have the authority to make decisions regarding their life, finances, and medical care. If they require support there is supported decision making, conservatorship or guardianship considered.

In supported decision making, your loved one must be competent to understand the decision being made and its implications in order for these decisions to be legally binding. An alternative to this is conservatorship and limited conservatorship is a common model utilized by parents of a disabled adult child. However, their needs may evolve to require the consideration of a more restrictive environment.

What is Guardianship?

A legal procedure called guardianship is where someone (often a family member) seeks the court to declare that a person is incapable of successfully managing their affairs due to a disability. A guardian assumes the role of the person with special needs and makes decisions on their behalf.

Establishing guardianship can be a time-consuming and expensive process, so it's important not to rush the decision. In the prior life stage, conservatorship was discussed as a viable alternative and least restrictive environment for your loved one who may wish to maintain some degree of autonomy or independence. However, guardianship might be in scope in a change in circumstances.

Numerous guardianships exist depending on the needs of the person. In most cases, one individual can act as both the guardian of the property and the guardian of the individual. A property guardian makes judgments regarding a person's assets, income, possessions, government assistance, and other financial matters. A person's healthcare, housing, diet, attire, and other matters that impact them can all be decided by a guardian of the person.

WHY IS A GUARDIAN NEEDED FOR A PERSON WITH SPECIAL NEEDS?

Physical and mental disability or incapacity can involve serious and persistent conditions that severely restrict a person's abilities to care for themselves, express themselves verbally, work, and live freely. Such a limitation illustrates the need for a variety of therapies and assistance.

A legal guardian can make a wide range of personal and medical decisions for the person in their care. Conservatorship generally grants much more limited decision-making powers and it is easier for parents to obtain. As a result, conservatorship is often first explored as appropriate for your loved one in early years of his or her adult life.

A conservator usually only has the authority to pay bills, make investments and handle other financial matters if they are the conservator of the estate at all. On the other hand, guardianship is a complete transfer of control and power to the guardian over either the person, their estate, or both.

In recent decades, guardianship for people with special needs—physically or mentally—has come to be seen as a policy designed to limit the independence and well-being of the ward. As a result, guardianships are kept to a minimum in order to provide wards the maximum amount of choice over their life while also upholding their dignity and independence. Wards are free to provide as much of their own care as is physically and intellectually feasible given their circumstances, with the major focus being on their wishes.

WHAT ARE THE POWERS OF A GUARDIAN?

Guardians are only given the authority required to complete tasks that a person with special needs cannot complete on their own. These authorities may include:

- Ensuring the availability and upkeep of care for the ward
- Making financial and medical decisions for the ward
- Ensuring that enough educational and medical services are provided.
- Providing the court with information on the ward's health. Court updates include the ward's living situation, mental and physical health status as determined by medical exams and official records, a list of the services the ward receives, a description of the guardian's services, an accounting of the ward's financial assets, and any other information required to

be submitted to the court in order for it to determine the ward's status and the guardian's responsibilities.

Because they are not providing caregiving services, guardians are not expected to supervise a ward's life. However, care managers might be engaged to manage the day to care and activities of a ward. The cost of care management, along with the cost of guardianship can deplete assets very quickly. For this reason, courts supervise guardianship cases to be sure costs are reasonable and families often find private less costly alternatives.

HOW IS A GUARDIAN FOR A SPECIAL NEEDS PERSON CHOSEN?

A guardian must meet the requirements to be chosen. State-by-state requirements vary, but generally speaking, a guardian must be 18 years of age and a legal adult and cannot have a criminal history that includes a felony or a serious misdemeanor that suggests dishonesty (forgery, bribery, etc.). Of course, the guardian must not be someone with special needs themselves.

If the ward is able to articulate their wishes, the court will decide based on those requests. If the ward is unable to communicate its intentions, the court will reach a decision based on pre-incapacity papers such as a will, a durable power of attorney, or a nomination of a guardian by an adult. The courts often prefer to select parents, a spouse, adult children, brothers, sisters, or other family members if there is no permanent power of attorney available.

GOVERNMENT BENEFITS FOR PEOPLE WITH SPECIAL NEEDS

Even though it is crucial to protect your child's eligibility for support from the government, people should be aware of what government benefits are available to adults with special needs and when these benefits are available. Anyone interested in learning more about getting government benefits for an adult child with special needs should speak with an attorney or check the most recent eligibility information from each specific government program because these programs can be complicated and often change.

People with special needs have access to a wide range of government benefits, which differ greatly between states. Among the important programs are:

- **Medicare,** which is a health insurance program for seniors (65 and older), some individuals with special needs (under 65), and individuals with end-stage renal disease (permanent kidney failure treated with dialysis or a transplant)
- **Medicaid, or MediCal in California,** offers low-income people access to essential medical care. Additionally, the majority of states offer Medicaid "waiver" programs that cover residential, daycare, career, and other services.
- **Supplemental Security Income (SSI)** gives people with disabilities money for housing and food. An individual must have less than $2,000 in "countable assets" to be eligible.
- **Social Security Disability Insurance (SSDI)** mandates that applicants must have a disability that has prevented them from working for at least a year. Benefits are determined by a person's past income, the number of quarters of employment, and program contributions.
- **Disabled Adult Child (DAC),** which necessitates a finding that the participant's disability began before the age of 22, that the

individual is single, and that the participant has a disabled parent who is working or deceased and is eligible for Social Security benefits.
- **Supplemental Nutrition Assistance Program (SNAP/Food Stamps),** which has SSI-like eligibility requirements.
- **Section 8 Housing** helps low-income families, which may include those with special needs, pay their rent. A sliding scale that takes into account family size and income determines eligibility.

Medicare and SSDI are not means-based programs. In other words, there is no examination of your financial situation to ascertain if you meet the program's requirements based on your income or resources. Medicare is a type of government-sponsored health insurance for the aged and people with special needs, whereas SSDI is offered to persons, minors, or children with special needs whose parent has passed away, retired, or become disabled. A child with special needs under the age of 22 who is unemployed may be eligible for SSDI benefits based on the former earnings of his or her parents.

Both Medicaid/MediCal and SSI are means-based programs. Financial need is a criterion for participation in those programs, and beneficiaries must fulfill stringent standards before receiving benefits. Medicaid recipients may be eligible for in-home care, hospital and nursing home costs, as well as some housing benefits. A child with special needs may be eligible for SSI, SSDI, Medicaid, and Medicare all at once.

It's crucial to understand the difference between means-based and non-means-based programs. Given the high cost of long-term medical and nursing care, as well as the fact that these benefits significantly increase a special need person's capacity to receive care, anyone wishing to give an asset to a child with special needs may prevent that child from receiving benefits from means-based programs. However, creating a supplemental needs trust for a family member with special needs can help pay for their care without barring them from receiving SSI or Medicaid benefits.

Excluding a primary residence and car, an adult with special needs must currently own no more than $2,000 in assets to be eligible for SSI benefits, though the criteria should be regularly checked for modifications. There are also income limits that would cause a dollar-for-dollar reduction in SSI payments. Most importantly, there is a connection between Medicaid eligibility and SSI eligibility. To the extent they enjoy SSI payments of any amount, special needs individuals qualify for Medicaid. Medicaid/MediCal is an important benefit to maintain since it covers medical costs, nursing home care, and mental health services, as well as food stamps.

Another possible reduction in SSI is in the form of free food or rent, or in-kind support and maintenance (ISM). To the extent free rent or food is given, there could be up to a one third reduction in SSI payments. Furthermore, if such reductions cause SSI payments to be reduced to zero, Medicaid/MediCal benefits disappear also. This stresses the importance of working with experts when considering government benefits in the planning process for individuals with special needs.

It is important to note here disabled adult child support is considered income and a one third portion of court ordered payments can result in a reduction in social security. In the absence of a court ordered payment after the age of 18, some parents agree it is better to deposit what used to be considered child support into an ABLE account instead. However, if a court order is required, it is possible to also do a 3rd party assignment of payments to a special needs trust and it is recommended that families consult with tax and legal experts who are familiar with how to protect government benefits in cases regarding child support.

In addition, free rent is considered in kind support and maintenance which might reduce social security checks by one third. In addition, if rent is paid out of a special needs trust, it is considered in kind support and maintenance. All of this stresses the importance of working with special needs advisors who will attest to their fiduciary duty to protect government benefits.

Many of the benefits covered under Medicaid are not covered via Medicare. Although supplemental needs trusts can help pay for additional care above and beyond what the government may supply, it is imperative to protect eligibility for Medicaid/MediCal for the in-home care and nursing care benefits as well as nutrition programs such as CalFresh in California.

Establishing a special needs estate plan including the appointment of successor trustees, a conservator in the event of future incapacity, or a standby guardian for a family member with developmental disabilities is also crucial. Additionally, you should have living wills, durable powers of attorney, and other similar documents. Finally, receiving government benefits can help a child with special needs acquire the means to pay for high-quality long-term care. It cannot be emphasized enough to protect these benefits as the number one priority.

TRANSITION SERVICES FOR ADULTS

Transition planning is an important aspect of this life stage and there is much to be considered. The goal of transitional services for adults with special needs is to teach them how to get ready for life after high school.

Some children with special needs finish high school at age 18 with the necessary skills and go on to succeed in their lives. Other children will require more support than what the general education curriculum provides, particularly as they leave school and enter adulthood. These are called adult transition programs.

There aren't enough hours in the school day for children with disabilities to receive the job-skills assistance they may require while still completing the standard curriculum. Some children will require assistance in locating a college that matches their unique set of skills. Some children need to develop life skills in order to succeed in the work world, such as how to prepare a meal, manage a checkbook, and interact with others.

Your child should ideally start getting these services at a young age. In middle school, some children might start receiving vocational (career) training. Others may decide to continue after receiving a certificate of attendance and enroll in an "18+" or "Transition" program rather than receiving a diploma.

Your child is entitled to receive assistance from the school system if they are receiving special education services, and it is specified in their Individualized Education Program (IEP). Even if they earned a certificate of attendance at the age of 18, your child could be entitled to continue receiving services until they generally turn 22.

A significant portion of the special education curriculum includes transition services. School districts must offer them in accordance with the Individuals with Disabilities Education Act (IDEA). If the Admission, Review, and Dismissal (ARD) committee determines that a transition plan is required, special education students must have one as part of their IEP by the age of 14 years old.

However, don't stress if your child is becoming older and you haven't begun to consider their transition. Move forward from wherever you are after taking a deep breath. It was not until just before Adam's senior year that we were offered a transition program for him, specifically the deaf. However, we had the rest of the school year to get him ready for that transition.

TRANSITION PLANNING FOR STUDENTS WITH SPECIAL NEEDS

As your loved one approaches graduation, there are several questions to consider while determining the right transition program to place him or her in.

- Is your child interested in attending college?
- Will your child enter the workforce right away? If so, what expertise will be required to carry out that work?
- When will your child graduate? Will it be at ages 18, 19, or perhaps 22 when students are no longer eligible for services from the school?
- What sort of diploma does your child want to obtain? Their college selections and classroom adjustments may be influenced by the diploma they choose.

Providing the relevant information can help your child receive the appropriate IEP and transition plan to assist them in developing post-high school goals.

18+ OR TRANSITION SERVICES YOU MIGHT FIND IN YOUR CHILD'S SCHOOL DISTRICT

To assist students who graduate or earn a certificate of attendance in place of graduation, some school systems provide 18+ and transition programs. Many also provide vocational training programs to assist students in choosing a career, getting work experience, and learning job skills.

Admission to these programs might be challenging. There are various rules in different school districts. The ARD committee for your child must decide whether to include these services in the IEP.

It's possible that some of these vocational courses will be offered at your child's high school or at the local community college. Classes may also be held at a specialized vocational school in some districts. Both professional classes and those that teach particular skills are typically included in these programs.

Titles of study programs could include:

- Business Education.
- Agricultural Science and Technology Education.
- Health Science Technology Education.
- Technology Education.

- Family and Consumer Sciences Education.
- Industrial Technology.
- Trade and Industrial Education.
- Marketing Education.
- Military Science Education.

Your child's school system can also put you in touch with local programs and organizations that can support their transition.

These could be one of these:

- Supported employment.
- Work-study programs.
- Particular training initiatives offered by the Texas Workforce Commission.
- Post-graduation initiatives that support your child's independence and college enrollment.

You can check the district website, contact the special education contact person, or try to get in touch with other parents in your region to learn more about the services your school system provides.

Keep in mind that your child is entitled to transition assistance that:

- Aim for results.
- Put more effort into raising your child's skills and grades.
- Facilitate your child's transition from school to after-school activities.
- Are centered on the particular needs of your child.
- Include career skills and growth, life objectives, and experience in the community.
- Consider your child's strengths, preferences, and interests.

Planning Considerations

This is the time in your loved one's life stage that your thinking shifts to matters of your loved one's financial future and estate matters. Special needs planning becomes front and center as you plan for the future. This is the life stage Adam, and I were at the release of the first edition of this book. It is a scary time of change for us, but it is written most, "do not be afraid". I will certainly try but I cannot promise that I will never worry.

Although you do not have a crystal ball for the future, you know that you must engage in longer-term planning for the future for your one at this life stage if you have not done so already. And, as you can see, there is a wide range of experts you will interact with. The quality of your outcomes will depend on your advisors' specialization in special needs disciplines.

The planning at this stage of life is beyond financial and your best choice in advisors are those who have skin in the game as fiduciaries who are willing to attest to their fiduciary obligations to defray expenses and mitigate risk. Advisors must be willing do the extra work required for special needs clients. Picking a designated Chartered Special Needs Consultant, ChSNC®, advisor is a good start to finding an expert who understand the totality of the challenges you are solving for.

This is the last life stage you have to impact your child's levels of development and resulting quality of life through educational resources. Resource planning, transition planning and vocational planning are areas of need that take priority here. All of this must be done at the same time that financial and estate planning addresses contingencies. There is a lot going on and engagement with advisors with the appropriate levels of expertise and empathy is more important than ever.

7

ACHIEVING INDEPENDENCE AS AN ADULT

For children with special needs or disabilities, there are numerous options available. Parents can often get therapies, aides, and tutors through the local school district. While this is fantastic for children in school, there is an issue when the child ages out of the educational system at 22 and is no longer eligible to receive these services. Due to this, many parents are at a loss as to how to help their child or where to turn for assistance.

Navigating this new stage of life can be frightening and daunting when parents suddenly lose all the support and guidance their child has had throughout their childhood. You only need to know where to go. The good news is that there are assistance and resources available for adults with special needs.

WHAT PARENTS SHOULD KNOW WHEN A CHILD WITH SPECIAL NEEDS TURNS 22

Even though it may be emotionally challenging for us, as parents, we want our children to grow up and leave the coop to live on their own as fully grown, independent adults. However, if you have a child with special needs, these worries can be more serious, and that objective might appear elusive or even unattainable. Because of this, parents should begin planning for their child with special needs' futures far in advance before the age of 22, regardless of how young the children may be.

The first thing to think about is what your child with special needs will do after graduating from high school. Can she attend college? Will he enroll in a trade school? Will she be independent? All of these discussions need to happen right away. Here are some of the things to consider when preparing for your child's special needs in the future.

Obtaining Conservatorship or Guardianship

As was mentioned in the previous chapter, if your child has health problems, you might want to think about requesting guardianship because, once your child with special needs turns 18, HIPAA, the 1996

Health Insurance Portability and Accountability Act, may prevent you as the parent from having access to his medical records. Parents or other caregivers do not necessarily have the right to see a patient's medical records if the patient is over the age of 18, as per HIPAA. Obtaining conservatorship or guardianship, ensures you will continue to be your child's legal guardian even when he is old enough to be considered an adult. This is the most impactful way to get around HIPPA if your child is unable to care for himself.

The court must be petitioned during the legal process of obtaining conservatorship or guardianship. An application must first be completed by parents to certify that their child does, in fact, have a disability, and a form must be submitted by a doctor to confirm this. Additionally, the applicant must explain why the child with special needs is unable to take care of himself. The process will then involve a hearing in front of a judge; therefore, it could be beneficial to work with a special needs attorney.

Due to budgetary restrictions, the government's assistance is actually decreasing; thus, it's crucial to have a special needs trust to pay for items that enhance a disabled person's quality of life. Creating a special needs trust as an additional source of funding to cover expenses such as services not covered by Medicaid that are not covered by government benefits.

In addition, if there is child support beyond the age of 18, it would be considered income to your disabled adult child. This was discussed in the prior life stage also. For payments beyond the age of 18, consider establishing an ABLE account to receive support payments that would otherwise result in a reduction in government benefits for individuals who receive SSI payments. To the extent a court order is involved, it is also possible to deposit support payments to a special needs trust. Needless to say, again, tax and legal experts must be consulted who are familiar with government benefits and how to protect them.

This is also the life stage when a parent might retire and begin to receive social security payments at retirement age. Disabled Adult Child (DAC) benefits might be requested. However, it is important to consider these payments will be dollar for dollar reduction in SSI payments. There are waivers for Medicaid/MediCal benefits if SSI goes to zero, but it is important to engage an expert in matters such as this to gain an understanding on benefits that are available and what might impact entitlement to them.

Pursuing Higher Education

Children have a right to a free, suitable public education under the IDEA, and schools are required to give them a quality education through the 12th grade. Some of the 13 different types of disabilities that the IDEA covers include autism, deafness, orthopedic disability, and visual impairment. Educational services can extend for special needs consumers up to the age of 22 years old.

An Individualized Education Program, which is a written description of your child's disability and how the school will support her, is given to children and young adults with special needs as part of the IDEA. The IEP will outline the child's academic progress, educational objectives, and transition strategies to help him get ready for life beyond high school.

Children with special needs are highly encouraged to either seek higher education or a vocational program if they are able to. Many advocates would advise a child with special needs to enroll in a small liberal arts institution since it will be less intimidating and more structured than a major university. Trade schools are another option, to the extent they offer career and technical education. In all cases, the ability to interact with peers and role models who are not special is crucial for an individual with special needs.

Choosing a Residence

The location of your child with special needs' home is another important decision to make when he or she is no longer considered a child. Parents often keep their children at home, but this has the drawback of not preparing them for independent living.

According to statistics, the child will survive parents and caregivers. Many children, even those with Down syndrome and other special needs, are now able to have complete or almost full lives, unlike in the past when children with special needs did not have a normal, usual life expectancy.

Parents should therefore think about assisting their child with special needs in finding a residence close to his medical professionals. We advise locating a specialist with extensive experience in the field and building a long-lasting relationship with the physician. The earlier you prepare for this, the fewer unexpected events you'll encounter along the route.

AGEING OUT OF ELIGIBILITY FOR SPECIAL EDUCATION

After receiving a conventional high school diploma, a student with an individualized education plan (IEP) loses their eligibility for special education and related services the month he or she turns 22. A general educational development (GED) certificate or a certificate of completion of high school is not equivalent to a "normal high school diploma," and neither of these alternative school credentials results in the termination of special education eligibility.

According to the California Association of Health and Education Linked Professions JPA (www.cahelp.org), when a student who is receiving special education support and services through an IEP, or a student who was found to be qualified for special education services before turning 19 is unable to obtain a "regular high school diploma" as described by Education Code 56026.1, they may be qualified to continue receiving special education and related services after turning 19. The oldest age at which a student may be eligible for special education is set by both California law and the federal IDEA. "Aging out" refers to the cessation of eligibility as a result of attaining the maximum age.

Both the federal Individuals with Disabilities Education Act (IDEA) and California law have maximum age limits for special education eligibility. The termination of eligibility, if a regular diploma has not been granted, for special education services, generally ends the month they turn 22. The child is then no longer eligible for special education on a permanent basis. According to Education Code Section 56026(c)(4) (A-C):

- Any participant in a program covered by this section who turns 22 between the months of January and June, inclusive, may continue to take part in that program through the end of the current fiscal year, including any extended school year programs for people with special needs established in accordance with Sections 3043 and 300.106 of Title 5 of the California Code of Regulations.
- Unless the person would otherwise finish their personalized education program at the end of the current fiscal year, any participant in a program under this act who turns 22 during the months of October, November, or December is terminated from the program on December 31 of the current fiscal year.

- If a participant turns 22 in July, August, or September of a new fiscal year, they will not be permitted to start that fiscal year's program, even if they are otherwise eligible to do so under this part. However, if a student is enrolled in a year-round program and is finishing their IEP during a term that overlaps with the start of a new fiscal year, they are permitted to do so.

Referring back to the CAHELP website, California law is very explicit that school districts cannot create an IEP to extend a student's eligibility past the date on which they would otherwise age out of special education or extend eligibility for students who are already aging out of special education. According to Education Code 56026(c)(4)(D):

- No local educational agency may create an individualized education program that extends these eligibility dates, and a student may never be required or permitted to attend school under the terms of this part beyond these eligibility dates solely on the grounds that the individual has not achieved his or her goals or objectives.

HOUSING OPTIONS FOR ADULTS WITH SPECIAL NEEDS

Fifty years ago, most people with even mild special needs spent their whole adult lives in institutions. Today, the majority of people with special needs, including those with extremely severe special needs, live in some kind of communal setting, in part due to cultural changes and decades of legal action.

In reality, the U.S. Supreme Court has held expressly that those receiving government benefits who have special needs must be accommodated in the least restrictive environment. The most well-liked housing options for adults with special needs are shown below.

Residing with one's parents or other relatives

Young adults with special needs often reside with their parents or other family members. Individuals with special needs who live with their parents avoid the somewhat tumultuous process of moving into a different form of home as adults and are typically cared for by family members who are familiar with their particular special needs. Medicaid funding can often be used to pay relatives who look after children in their parent's homes.

Staying with one's parents is not always a good option, as any young adult will undoubtedly explain to you at some point. Sometimes a child's special needs will be greater than the parents are able to handle. In other situations, a child's parents might have a negative influence on him, might even maltreat him, or might steal his government payments. If a person with special needs is always surrounded by the same family members, depending on their level of social engagement, they may not have the chance to meet many other individuals.

Additionally, as parents age, it may become impossible for them to care for their children any longer, and the child may experience more trauma than if they had left when they were younger because they are leaving their longtime home.

It is important to note here, again, that free rent is considered in kind support and maintenance (ISM). This type of support is counted as resources in the eyes of the social security administration and it could cause a one third reduction in SSI payments.

To avoid an ISM penalty reduction in SSI payments, many adults with disabilities pay rent even to family members under a lease agreement. Hopefully, this is an aspect of special needs planning that was addressed in the prior life stage.

Lastly, fiduciary advisors should be aware that rent may not come out of a special needs trust without an IHSM penalty. However, it may come out of an ABLE account or the checking account SSI payments are direct deposited into.

Section 8 Housing

People with low incomes can purchase housing in the neighborhood with the help of the Section 8 program's vouchers. A Section 8 user typically spends about one-third of their monthly income on rent, with the remaining costs covered by the voucher.

A large number of people with special needs who rely solely on Supplemental Security Income (SSI) or Social Security Disability Insurance (SSDI) benefits are probably also eligible for Section 8. Theoretically, Section 8 landlords must adhere to specific requirements in order to rent their properties to Section 8 tenants, but in practice, this is rarely thoroughly inspected.

People with low earnings and mild to moderate special needs may be able to live independently in the community with the help of Section 8 vouchers. However, obtaining a Section 8 voucher typically takes years, and if one is obtained, there could not be any Section 8 rental units available in the person's neighborhood.

Additionally, Section 8 housing is inappropriate for those with more complex special needs who are unable to live independently.

Supportive Housing/Group Homes

Living in supportive group homes alongside other individuals who have special needs is a popular choice for many people with disabilities. Depending on the program, these residences might have counselors, and other staff members who help the residents with surviving independently, or the residents might live independently in some situations. There are different types of group homes, and there are many different means to pay for them, including private money or governmental programs for people with disabilities.

For those with exceptional needs who don't need more intensive care but can't live independently, group homes are fantastic possibilities. Group homes may also provide a social environment that residents do not have if they live with their parents or on their own.

Assisted Living Facilities

Some people with special needs, particularly elderly people, reside in institutions for assisted living. Assisted living facilities often house individuals in their own apartments within a building or group of buildings, despite the fact that the word "assisted living" has grown to signify a variety of things. The residents have the option of cooking in their apartments or dining in a common dining room. They also receive non-skilled care in their apartments, such as help with bathing, cleaning, and occasionally administering medication.

Dementia and other neurological diseases are treated at some assisted living homes.

Nursing Homes (Skilled Nursing Facilities)

If it is hard to provide 24-hour expert medical care for a person with special needs at home, the person may need to live in a skilled nursing facility. For most families, nursing homes are a last resort, but in some situations, they may be the best choice for a person with severe special needs because of the constant supervision of care and the fact that the person's family members do not have to devote their entire lives to caring for their loved one.

Facilities for skilled nursing are very pricey, often costing more than $10,000 per month. A person with significant special needs who has few assets may often be eligible for Medicaid coverage, which will cover the cost of their care in a skilled nursing facility.

Special Needs Trust Home Ownership/Rent Payment

Special needs Trusts may purchase a home for their beneficiaries or provide funds to cover the rent of an individual flat. Since the trust can also pay for services to support the recipient's independent living, this is often a very flexible option for the beneficiary. However, a trust's homeownership comes with a sizable number of obligations such as repairs & maintenance, association payments, property taxes, and homeowner's insurance that should be considered.

Some parents chose to purchase a home in the name of their loved one outright to protect their loved one from losing their home when they are gone. Since a residence and a car are exempt from means testing for SSI or Medicaid/MediCal, the fully paid house and car may remain in the adult child's name without impacting government benefits. This is another area to consult with an expert who is knowledgeable on special needs subjects such as the purchase of a residence and car for your loved one.

FINANCIAL PLANNING FOR YOUR LOVED ONE WITH SPECIAL NEEDS

All parents worry about their children's futures, but it's reasonable to worry more when your child has severe medical requirements or disabilities. For instance:

- What kind of life will my child wish to lead, and where?
- How can I ensure that costs (such as rent and transportation) are covered if my child is unable to work?
- How can I save money for the future of my child without affecting government benefits?

You could struggle to sleep if you have questions like these. However, according to experts, making a strategy helps reduce anxiety. The following ten stages will help you plan your child's financial future. Some are easy; some are difficult; some are free, and some need money for legal services. Start working on some of these at this life stage, to the extent you need to create or update the special needs plan for the future of your loved one.

1. Create a Special Needs Trust and an ABLE Account

The long-term financial strategy for your child should include a special needs trust. You can use this account to deposit money that you have saved, presents that others have given to your child, and any insurance payouts that may have been received. The eligibility of your child for government benefits like Medicaid and Supplemental Security Income won't be affected by this trust because it is exempt from means testing.

Even if you are currently unable to contribute to a trust, you can nonetheless establish one. Making the trust the beneficiary of your estate and life insurance policy will prevent your child from inheriting those assets in the event of your passing. Why wouldn't you want your child to receive your estate as a beneficiary? Because if your child has more than $2,000 in assets, they may not be eligible for federal programs like SSI.

Create an **ABLE** account as another way to plan for your child's financial future. According to the Achieving a Better Life Experience (ABLE) Act of 2014, states are able to designate a tax-advantaged savings program for people with disabilities to use to pay for eligible disability costs tax-free. Your child can receive up to $15,000 annually for all contributions combined with an ABLE account, and the money grows tax-free.

2. Create a Living Trust and a Will

What will happen to your possessions after you pass away is specified in living trust and in a will. In addition to a living trust, you can ensure that your assets go to the special needs trust and not your child by making a will naming a special needs trust (SNT) as the beneficiary of estate assets that are not held in trust. Living trust beneficiary designations should also result in assets passing to a SNT versus directly to your loved one. Without a will, a judge in probate court may designate your child as a beneficiary, which may prevent that child from receiving government benefits. You can name a guardian to look after your child in your living trust or will as well.

Making a trust or a will should not be a DIY project when you have a child with special needs. Hire a lawyer that specializes in representing people with disabilities and is familiar with the disability laws in your state. After the paperwork is prepared, have your attorney keep one and distribute copies to any executors or guardians of the will names. For a recommendation to an attorney in your state, get in touch with the Special Needs Alliance or the Academy of Special Needs Planners.

3. Choose a Guardian

If you are gone before your child reaches adulthood, a guardian will take care of them. Think about how much time you now devote to taking care of your child's requirements while choosing this person. Who has that kind of commitment under control? To whom has your child formed a bond? Who possesses the perseverance, understanding, and other character attributes required to handle the ongoing obligations of raising your child?

Once you've chosen someone, find out if they'll take on that duty (even though you hope it will never be necessary). And mention how this dedication probably won't end when your child turns 18.

4. Choose a Trustee

After your passing, a trustee will be in charge of overseeing trust assets including the special needs trust. It could be a close relative, a close friend, an impartial professional trustee, a bank, or even a lawyer. The trustee makes sure that the funds in the trust are exclusively used for your child and only for the services you've designated or that are necessary to meet your child's requirements. The trustee also oversees the investments made using the trust's funds. In addition, the guardian of your child may not be permitted to spend any funds from the trust without the trustee's consent.

A word about trustees and guardians: They often aren't the same people, and some financial consultants advise against having them ever be the same person. You can provide a "checks and balances" mechanism for your child's future requirements by dividing these jobs.

5. Increase Your Savings

Parents of a child with special needs quickly come to realize that just because a child requires a particular therapy or treatment doesn't mean that your school system will provide it or that your insurance will pay for it. Savings from one's own resources are crucial in this situation. Start saving as much as you can each month — no sum is too little — to pay for these additional costs. Don't ever put this money in your child's name, please.

Savings can also be used to cover expenses like hiring a special needs advocate. This is a specialist in special education who can guide you through the paperwork, initiatives, and legal requirements that have an impact on the services your child is eligible for. It is recommended to get in touch with your state's special education advocacy group first, such as your neighborhood Family Voices branch. If you require assistance beyond what these organizations can provide, think about working with a special needs advocate. In the long run, special needs advocates help parents save money by ensuring that children receive all the services to which they are legally entitled from their local school district.

Ask for recommendations from other parents of children with special medical needs or contact your neighborhood school system to locate an advocate in your region. Reach out to local colleges with disability programs or groups that focus on your child's disability.

6. Write a Letter of Intent

It's crucial to plan for your child's financial future. But so is ensuring that, in the event that something happens to you, your child's basic requirements would be covered. A letter of intent can help with that. Is the daily schedule of your child particularly important? Put it in writing and be as specific as you can. The daily, weekly, and monthly timetables for your child are all the same. Include things that your child enjoys and dislikes as well as helpful local resources.

Make a list of your child's doctors, therapists, and other medical support personnel, along with their current medications, dosages, and timetables. Are there individuals or activities you want to keep away from your child? Also, write that down.

After that, update the letter once a year. You can write this paper yourself because it is not a formal legal document. Keep one of each wherever you have copies of your estate planning documents. Additionally, make sure a copy is sent to the designated guardian of your child.

7. Create an independence plan for your child

Start planning where your child will live as an adult when they are around 14 years old. You must register your child with the developmental disabilities office of your state in order for them to be eligible for placement in a group home as an adult. Furthermore, the earlier you register, the better, as the waitlist for placement in a group home might be up to ten years long.

People with disabilities typically become ineligible for education programs provided by the local public school system when they are 21 or 22 years old. After high school, children can enroll in college or a trade school, find employment, or engage in voluntary work. Programs for young adults in many towns offer basic skills like cooking, housekeeping, job training, and financial literacy. Speak with the local Office of Vocational Rehabilitation or your guidance counselor at school to find out what programs are offered in your region.

8. Make a conservatorship or power of attorney application

Children who turn 18 are considered legal adults. Your child now has the authority to make financial and medical decisions. Take into consideration becoming your child's conservator or legal guardian if they are unable to. This enables you to continue exercising the same levels of oversight and judgment as when your child was younger.

Consider a power of attorney and a health care proxy if your child can make certain decisions but still needs your direction in regard to finances, legal matters, and medical care.

To assist with this process, it is best to hire an attorney. This will guarantee that you have all the authority you would require to take over your adult child's medical care in an emergency. If your child is unable or unwilling to consent to you having power of attorney, the issue will probably be decided in front of a probate court judge.

9. Educate Your Family

You could wish to ask your grandparents, aunts, uncles, and other family members for financial assistance. However, make sure they understand why nothing should be put in your child's name. Have a family gathering and explain why Grandpa can't make your child the beneficiary of his life insurance policy or leave your child anything in his will. Nothing should ever be given in your child's name, whether it be a cash present or a savings bond, stock, or other assets.

Family members are free to leave something to your child if they so choose. To ensure that your child has no assets of their own, however, advise them to name the special needs trust as the beneficiary or suggest that they make a donation to the child's ABLE account.

A 529 savings plan is not necessary if your child is not going to college. Private schools, tutoring, or therapies required before the age of 18 are not permitted to be paid for with those funds; only postsecondary education is permitted.

10. Need Support? Find a Consultant

A professional financial planner or special needs financial planner can assist if all of this is too much. Ask your human resources department if this service is provided by your employer as a part of your benefits package. For a recommendation to a specialist in your region, you may also contact the Special Needs Alliance or the Academy of Special Needs Planners.

Planning Considerations

Collaboration across environments shifts to include coping strategies as your child ages our of educational or transitional services. The realization of adulthood might be devastating, and it is important to help your loved one cope with such a significant shift in lifestyle. Planning at life stage is to minimize disruption while maximizing your loved one's quality of life as an adult while you are here and beyond. Helping families at this life stage centers around lifetime planning strategies for special needs consumers and helping them cope with significant life changes beyond prior life stages.

Planning is beyond financial at this life stage and this is the stage most parents are the most afraid of. Uncertainty of the future of your loved one at a time when you are not there to help is a valid concern for any reasonable parent of a loved one with special needs. Needless to say, nobody wants to leave a loved one alone or without support.

For me, this is where my faith comes in. I cannot know the future with certainty, and God does not want me to. I must rely on God to guide me and Adam to the resources he would have us enjoy as we strive to live in alignment with His will for us. This has been mu daily prayer for Adam since he was diagnosed.

It is comforting to know my prayer will remain for Adam even when I am gone and, in the heavens, watching over him from above. Planning for the future is good. Trying to control every aspect of the future is not.

Please remember, God has this and so do you.

WARRIOR PARENTS

To the parent who drives her child to ABA therapy while her friends drop off their children at soccer practice, you're not alone. To the mother who is always carrying a PECS book, a salute to you!

To the dad who avoids milestone discussions with his friends because his child is years behind, your child is great just the way he is.

To the mother who was embarrassed by her son's screaming at the grocery store, I've been there, too.

To the parent who is scouring the internet for the right kind of therapy for her child, you are your child's best advocate.

To the dad who is reluctant to take his child to restaurants, parks, or other public places, I understand it's challenging.

To the mother who is still lamenting the loss of her dream of taking her son to the movies or baseball practice, it might not turn out the way you imagined it, but it will turn out fine.

To the father who felt foolish for celebrating after his son requested bubbles by saying "buh," every single accomplishment is worthy of celebration, crack open the champagne!

To the mom holding back her tears after another treatment report that makes her feel like her child isn't improving, don't give up hope!

To the father who desires for his daughter to talk, you are not alone.

You are not alone! We are not alone. Remember that you're not alone when you're trying to keep going or when it seems hopeless. I want you to keep in mind that you're doing a fantastic job when you feel like no one sees you unless your child is crying or when you're unsure of how you're going to manage it any longer. You are doing your best to raise your child, and I know you adore them. Remember that I understand what you're going through and that there are many more like us out there when you feel like no one else does.

We all experience bad days; therefore, it's fine. You are fantastic, and your child understands it even if he or she is unable to express it to all the parents out there who are making every effort to provide their children the best life they can, despite the obstacles. I salute you!

There is no universal response to this question, just as no two children are alike. The difficulties a child faces could be caused by physical, developmental, behavioral, or mental health problems. For the parents of the child, each of these situations raises a variety of worries: Am I doing enough? Will my child be alright? Why is this happening?

Feelings of isolation, despair, resentment, and hopelessness might result from the uncertainty and hardships. We find comfort and hope when we acknowledge our emotions and give them to God. We can ponder God's whereabouts and what He might have to say about raising a child with special needs.

The solution is revealed when we turn to God's word. To that end, the fourteen verses below might help parents develop a mindset resulting in seven attitudes we might cultivate to help ourselves and our loved ones:

1. Gratitude and Intention

"For You knit me together inside my mother's womb; You made my innermost parts. I shall give gratitude to You since Your works are lovely and my spirit is completely aware of how awesome and wonderfully fashioned, I am" (Psalm 139:13-14).

"Give thanks in all circumstances because God's will for you in Christ Jesus is that you do so" (1 Thesselonians 5:18).

The verse emphasizes the value of thankfulness. Joy happens when we concentrate on our blessings. This is a lovely way to live in general, and it's even more crucial if you have a child with special needs. We can be thankful for God's unending love and the understanding that we are his creation, even in the worst, most trying times.

According to 1 Thessalonians 5:18, it is the Lord's desire that we give thanks in all circumstances. He gives us instructions for our benefit rather than His own. The happiness we experience when we practice thankfulness improves our mindset and helps us be better disciples and parents.

2. Set priorities

"As they proceed with their journey, He entered a village, where a woman by the name of Martha invited Him into her home. She also had a sister named Mary, who was sitting at the Lord's feet and hearing what He had to say. However, Martha was preoccupied with all of her preparations and approached Him, saying, 'Lord, do You not mind that my sister has left me to do the serving alone? then request that she assist me.' But the Lord said, Mary has chosen a great part, which shall not be taken away from her, but Martha, Martha, you are troubled and distracted by many things, just one of which is vital." (Luke 10:38-42).

"But put God's kingdom and righteousness first, and everything else will be given to you" (Matthew 6:33).

To-do lists and everyday tasks are often made more difficult or tough for families with a child with special needs. Decide what really has to be done each morning and concentrate on those tasks. As parents, we have a lot of responsibilities to juggle throughout the day, including jobs, cleaning, social engagements, and bill payment. However, raising our children is the most crucial task of all. It might be challenging to tune out the noise and visuals that the outside world bombards us with in order to concentrate on the things that God has placed in our life. Be encouraged by the knowledge that the love we demonstrate for others around us, especially for our children, will have a much longer-lasting effect than a spotless home or a popular Instagram post.

Likewise, we need to make time for ourselves and our spiritual connection with God. We cannot pour from an empty cup. We can best serve people when we carve out time for prayer and meditation. This enables us to give to others from our overflow and I believe this is what God intended for us.

A stronger foundation in my faith is also what Adam has taught me. He has an unfiltered seat closer to God that blesses everyone who encounters him. He is a "royal soul". If we stay focused and centered on what is important in life, everything falls into place and we experience an abundance of miracles. Glory be.

3. Support and Community

"Two heads are always better than one because they get more out of their work because if one falls, the other will help him up. But woe to the one who trips and cannot be picked up by another! Furthermore, two can stay warm if they lie down together, but how can one stay warm by themselves? And if one can defeat a lone opponent, two can struggle against him. Three-stranded cords do not easily break apart" (Ecclesiastes 4:9-12).

"In the presence of the Lord, humble yourselves, and He will elevate you" (James 4:10).

God did not make us go through life by ourselves. We shouldn't be reluctant to receive the love and support of our extended family, friends, churchgoers, and coworkers while we are going through any kind of adversity. Accepting offers of babysitting, housekeeping assistance, or company during a tiresome and stressful doctor's appointment is not a show of weakness.

Because we believe no one could ever understand the tests we face on a daily basis as parents of children with special needs, there are times when we are reluctant to share our experiences with others. We might also be concerned about being judged. However, the truth is that when we are open and honest, it encourages people to share their own struggles, even if they are not the same as ours. Sharing our challenges with one another helps us grow. Fellowship and healing are made possible by humility.

4. Resilience

"He who controls his spirit is better than he who captures a city, and he who is slow to wrath is better than the mighty" (Proverbs 16:32).

"Let's not lose heart in doing good; for when the time is right, we shall reap, if we do not get weary" (Galatians 6:9).

Patience appears to be a quality that is underestimated in our fast-paced culture and is often even seen as a sign of weakness. However, the knowledge of God teaches us something very different regarding patience. Parenting, especially if your child has special needs, will put the ultimate test on your patience and help you to develop it. A calm attitude in the midst of a storm, no matter what form it takes, is one of the greatest things you can have.

Even though our days might seem to have produced little, if we were able to maintain our composure while dealing with a difficult situation involving our child, we had made significant progress. Although it can seem like we barely made it through the crisis, we can be confident that the love we have sown into the heart of our child has left a long-lasting impression.

5. Don't be anxious

"The birds neither sow nor reap nor collect into barns; however, your heavenly Father provides for them. Are you really not worth much more than they are?" (Matthew 6:26.)

"Have I not ordered you? Be fearless and strong. The Lord, your God, will be with you wherever you go, so do not be afraid or disheartened" (Joshua 1:9).

All parents experience anxiety, but parents of children with special needs experience it significantly more. In addition to worrying about our children's immediate needs, we might also worry about what the future may hold for them. What obstacles will they be able to surmount? How will they behave as adults? When we pass away, who will look after them?

Numerous verses in the Bible warn us not to be afraid or concerned about anything, no matter what the situation. It's natural to experience anxiety and fear, but if we concentrate on how much God loves us—and our child—we may summon the confidence to make decisions based on faith rather than fear. We have peace and can be the parents God created us to be because we know God is with us and will take care of the problems that are beyond our control.

6. Discipline with Wisdom and Love

"Train up a child in the way he should go. Even as he gets older, he won't give up on it" (Proverbs 22:6).

"Fathers, train up your children in the discipline and instruction of the Lord and do not provoke your children to anger" (Ephesians 6:4).

I used to believe that Proverbs 22:6 simply referred to bringing up children in accordance with biblical principles. But God is far more intelligent and compassionate than to use a one-size-fits-all approach to parenting. Although this passage of Scripture implies that parents should bring up their children to follow the Lord, the phrase "in the path he should go" actually means "according to the dictates of his way." God has given every one of our children with exceptional needs certain distinctive strengths. They must also overcome difficulties and flaws. Making a child the best version of themselves and assisting them in choosing wisely for the rest of their lives is our responsibility as parents.

In addition to becoming irritated and more inclined to lose our temper, trying to make our children into someone they are not will prevent them from following the route God has for them in life. We can preserve order and structure with our children with special needs while also letting them be and grow into who God made them to be with the aid of the Holy Spirit.

7. Be an Advocate

"Open your mouth for the voiceless, for the rights of all the disadvantaged" (Proverbs 31:8).

"One who thinks of the helpless is blessed; the Lord will deliver them in the day of need" (Psalm 41:1).

We must speak up for our children in a world where they might be misunderstood or not get the greatest medical care due to ignorance. It may be necessary to gently explain our child's conduct to a daycare employee in some cases, or it may be necessary to get a second or even third opinion from a medical expert. Don't give up when the solutions are difficult to uncover or look incorrect. Continue looking, getting information, and going for what's best for your child. Keep in mind that God is your advocate and that He is battling alongside you to ensure your child has the best possible future.

You are not alone in raising your child with special needs. In addition to the fact that you are not alone in your struggles as a parent, God is also by your side, supporting and loving you all the way. He is not an error-prone God. He was certain of your child's characteristics. He is aware of your identity and your potential when He is your leader. Hold fast to Him and let His love, understanding, and grace uplift and strengthen you as you navigate the parenting road.

CONCLUSION

For parents, having qualities like patience, awareness, and empathy are crucial for supporting children who face special difficulties. Additionally, raising well-adjusted and capable children depends greatly on fostering strong self-esteem and resilience. Additionally, parents must not misinterpret a child's avoidance or displeasure as being lazy or disobedient. It's crucial to keep in mind that children with special needs are motivated and often put in more effort than their classmates. In general, parents should pay close attention, listen, or take note of any difficulties a child may be having in their academic or social lives.

By enlisting outside assistance, families with young children can build a solid network of support. To effectively encourage your child's development, it is crucial to enlist the help of the appropriate individuals and experts. For instance, having positive relationships with teachers throughout the academic year can make it easier for parents to discuss any issues with their children straight immediately. Making a file with all interactions, interventions, reports, and information about a student's needs and development is a good suggestion if you want to have everything in one place for future reference.

In the end, parents must keep in mind that learning is a process and that developing any new ability will take time, especially if a child is lagging behind their peers. Although a child may not be hitting conventional milestones, given enough time and the correct intervention, they will probably succeed. It is crucial to empathize with the child and applaud victories, no matter how minor they may be.

My best piece of advice to parents is to adore their children for the unique, lovely beings they are. Keep your attention on their strengths and have faith that they will learn to manage, overcome, or cope with any differences they may have from other people with time and the correct sorts of support. Try your best to identify any potential weaknesses, issues, or disabilities they may have and offer the appropriate support for them.

However, try not to focus on their differences from what is considered to be "normal" to the point where you or your child loses sight of how wonderful they are at their core. Also, keep in mind that special learning needs change over time.

THE BIG LEAP FORWARD

This was written for a caregiver, Elizabeth, who Adam survived. I was compelled to read *The Big Leap: Conquer Your Hidden Fear and Take Life to the Next Level* by Gay Hendricks after Elizabeth's sudden passing. Since this book is about leaping from one life stage to the other, it is appropriate to remember Elizabeth here as she leaped forward to the spirit world.

We loved Elizabeth very much and within 7 days of her passing, I was traveling on business and delayed coming home until I finished the book title above. It was as if the delays were established to create the time and space for me to finish the book and gain the following insight, which I believe was directly from Elizabeth.

1. *Do not argue.*
2. *Do not withhold anything.*
3. *Do not control or dominate.*
4. *If you have to always be right, there is no room to be happy.*
5. *In relationship — we are always in them:*

    a. *Take time alone.*
    b. *Speak your truth.*
    c. *Feel your feelings.*
    d. *Be affectionate.*

6. *Rather than drinking or eating too much, or getting sick, or trying to escape intimacy through arguments or deflecting compliments, ground yourself in positive ways like:*

    a. *Earthly dancing.*
    b. *Earthly walking.*
    c. *Clean out your earthly belongings in cluttered areas.*
    d. *Sing and enjoy music and your garden.*

7. *And finally, be sweat to each other and to yourselves. We are all connected.*

This wisdom was familiar to me because on reading them, they reminded me of what Elizabeth embodied. She shared with me her prayer on entering our life: "God, let me be a blessing to this family". She brought her joy into our lives and we will forever be grateful for that.

Her funeral was delayed multiple times. Since I was not able to share this then, I dedicate this part of my book to Elizabeth and the many caregivers who came into our lives to help enable Adam to leap forward to life stages of his own that they were a part of. I will leave you with a couple of quotes from the book.

The Big Leap: Conquer Your Hidden Fear and Take Life to the Next Level by Gay Hendricks:

"Going forward on your path, may your every day be filled with much practical magic and everyday miracles. May you transcend each and every one of your limits, and long may you glide the high currents of love, abundance, and creative contribution."

"We can try with all our might to pretend we're separate from the rest of the universe, but one way or the other it will catch up to us and welcome us back into its embrace."

May the embrace of this book edify you and encourage you in your journey moving forward. God bless you and keep each and every one of you safe, healthy, happy and whole. Amen.

ABOUT THE AUTHOR

Kerrie A. Lloyd, ChSNC®

Kerrie is a family fiduciary and Chartered Special Needs Consultant (**ChSNC®**). Kerrie has held leadership positions with the most esteemed names in the financial services industry including State Street, Bank of New York Mellon, and Wells Fargo. Kerrie has also helped advisors build out their fiduciary practices serving families impacted by disabilities before opening up a practice of her own. Having worked with, institutional fiduciaries for over 25 years, she is in a unique position to help special needs fiduciaries serve consumers in a cost-efficient service model including improved risk management controls with daily operational oversight and governance.

Kerrie earned a Bachelor of Arts degree in Business Finance from California State University Fullerton where she also joined the National Financial Management Honors Society. Kerrie also earned her Chartered Special Needs Consultant (**ChSNC®**) designation in 2020 through fully accredited institution by the Middle States Commission of Higher Education. In 2019, Kerrie renewed her Series 7 and 66 licenses, and she earned her Life, Variable, Health & Accident insurance contracts license with the California Department of Insurance (license #0N08518).

In addition to her financial services career, Ms. Lloyd is the author of *Planning the Future for A Special Needs Child* and she has written multiple blogs. She is also the founder of Integrative Solution Services LLC, www.integrativesolutionservices.com, where she provides consulting and collaboration tools for the special needs community.

Kerrie is also a Doctor of Natural Health, NhD, and she is certified in Pivotal Response Therapy for Autism through the Koegel Autism Center at UC Santa Barbara (now at Stanford University). Ms. Lloyd is additionally a Self Determination Independent Facilitator through her completion of the California State Council of Developmental Disabilities (www.scdd.ca.gov) webinar series.

Kerrie also served on a regional oversight board for the for the California State Council for Developmental Disabilities (appointed by the Orange County Board of Supervisors) and she is a Past President and Board Member of the Los Angeles Chapter of the Western Pension & Benefits Conference. Kerrie continues to participate in industry conferences and symposiums throughout the United States where she is also asked to speak or moderate sessions for attendees.

RESOURCES

One Day My Soul Just Opened Up: 40 Days and 40 Nights Toward Spiritual; Strength and Personal Growth, Iyanla Vanzant

Special Diets for Special Kids, Lisa Lewis, Ph.D.

Overcoming Autism: Finding the Answers, Strategies, and Hope That Can Transform a Child's Life, Lynn Kern Koegel, Ph.D. and Claire LaZebnik

The Out of Sync Child: Recognizing and Coping with Sensory Processing Disorder, Carol Stock Kranowitz, M.A.

The Verbal Behavior Approach: How to Teach Children with Autism and Related Disorders, Mary Lynch Barbera with Tracy Rasmussen, Forward by Dr. Mark Sundberg

Healing ADD: The Breakthrough Program That Allows You to See and Heal the 7 Types of ADD, Daniel G. Amen, M.D.

Wrightslaw Special Education Law, Second Edition, Peter W.D. Wright, Esq. and Pamela Darr Wright, MA, MSW, Founders of the Wrightslaw Website

Special Education in Contemporary Society, Seventh Edition: An Introduction to Exceptionality, Richard M. Gargiulo and Emily C. Bouck

Growing Up on The Spectrum: Guide to Life, Love, and Learning for Teens and Young Adults with Autism and Asperger's, Lynn Kern Koegel, Ph.D. and Claire LaZebnik

Special Needs Trusts: Protect Your Child's Financial Future, Attorneys Kevin Urbatsch and Michelle Fuller-Urbatsch

Emotional Labor: Why a Woman's Work is Never Done and What To Do About It, Regina F. Lark, Ph.D., CPO with Judith Kolberg

The Big Leap: Conquer Your Hidden Fear and Take Lifwe to the Next Level, Gay Hendricks

Mother Warriors: A Nation of Parents Healing Autism Against All Odds, Jenny McCarthy

Please also visit www.integrativesolutionservices.com on the resources page for access to links to websites utilized in the writing of this book.

Printed in Great Britain
by Amazon

7518074b-9cd8-46c3-842e-088d695ab43bR02